ODYSSEY OF A CREATRESS

ODYSSEY OF A CREATRESS

A HEROINE'S JOURNEY TO UNCOVER THE ESSENCE OF HER FEMININE SOUL

MADELINE K. ADAMS

ROSLYN PUBLISHING

Copyright © Madeline K Adams, 2018

All rights reserved. This book or any portion thereof may not be reproduced, or used in any manner whatsoever, other than for 'fair use' as brief quotations embodied in articles and reviews, without prior written permission of the publisher.

The information given in this book should not be treated as a substitute for professional medical advice. Any use of information in this book is at the reader's discretion and risk. The intent of the author is only to offer information of a general nature to help the reader in their quest for soul wellbeing. Neither the author nor the publisher can be held responsible for any loss, claim, or damage arising out of the use, or misuse, of suggestions made, the failure to take medical advice, or for any material on third party websites.

First published 2018
A catalogue record of this book is held at the National Library of New Zealand
ISBN 978-0-473-42281-3 1st Edition
ISBN 978-0-473-50070-2 2nd Edition 2020
ISBN 978-0-473-50071-9 EPub

Roslyn Publishing
P O Box 32276
Auckland, 0744
New Zealand
www.sourceandsoul.com

For Marnie, Emelie and Sofia

CONTENTS

Introduction	xi

PART I
1. Taking a Leap	3
2. Intuition and Synchronicity	8
3. Becoming lost	14
4. Rennes-le-Château	20
5. Quillan at the Full Moon	25
6. Returning Home	28

PART II
7. The Myth of Psyche	35
8. Psyche's tasks	43
9. Nuances of a Heroine's journey	49

PART III
La Vierge Noire	59
10. La Vierge Noire	61
11. Qualities of the Dark feminine	71
12. The Moon's Light and her Darkness	79
Cave Dweller	87
13. Time in my Cave	88
14. Soul Languages	92

PART IV
The River Speaks	107
15. A Call to Return	109
16. Alet-les-Bains	117
17. Rennes-le-Château	122
18. Honouring the Black Virgin	128

PART V
The Sacred Creatrix 139
19. History: Her-Story 141
20. Living the Creatress 150
21. The Circle Completes 157
22. The Essence of Feminine Soul 165

Postscript: 173
Glossary 177
Acknowledgments 179
About the Author 181
Sources and Further Reading 183
Also by Madeline K. Adams 185
Afterword 187

*She gives herself permission to shine her light
And to withdraw her light into the realms of darkness
To renew herself in honour of the cycles of becoming
Which are the core of her creative essence*

INTRODUCTION

The *Odyssey of a Creatress* is my personal "soul story" ~ a mid-life wakeup call that becomes my heroine's quest, beginning with my wanderings in France. I am led into dark spaces and explore the subtle realms of feminine mystery; and I learn to become the Creatress of my life's story.

An "Odyssey" is a spiritual quest named after Odysseus. His story, immortalised in an epic Greek poem by Homer, tells of his 10-year journey to return to his kingdom of Ithaca after the Trojan wars. His experiences along the way transform him and he arrives home to his wife and family, a deeply changed man.

~

Mine is the story of a woman who set out in search of a place to call home. At the age of forty, finding myself divorced and disillusioned with my relationships, I began a five-month solo journey around the world, leaving my old life behind to begin a personal quest.

My journey has been long and I often walked my path alone, feeling lost and invisible to those around me. In hindsight, though, I see that my quest became my heroine's journey and morphed into an exploration of all that is essentially feminine.

∾

For the next many years, I would follow a path that wound its way like a river through the Greek myth of Psyche and the Black Virgin statues of France.

I met life's challenges and gained new understanding, and I learned a new way of making meaning of my life, and in time I began to mould a new vision that was motivated by the values and perceptions I had gained through my experiences. I began to uncover the pure essence of the feminine within me and to know the beauty of my soul.

It is only now, as I enter the third phase of my life, that I am able to understand the meanings of the powerful symbols that have guided me to uncover the elusive mystery of the feminine. The realisation came to me that I felt pregnant with a story that needed to be told and so I began to write about my experiences in France – how intuition became my guide, and how I learned to trust my inner wisdom. I didn't know at the time that it would become my odyssey, lasting twenty-two years that would culminate with me embracing the feminine archetype of the Creatress.

∾

My story begins in New Zealand. It was 1989, and I felt a call to begin a journey that would take me to a small village in the southwest of France. My experiences there would create a need for me to uncover a new awareness of my feminine energy. The ancient myth of Psyche would come to resonate within me and give me a greater understanding of my path and of the lessons that, as a heroine, I was called to learn.

While in France, I began to explore the statues of the Black Virgin and Child as a way to deepen my connection with the archetypal dark feminine. I was led into dark spaces where I found the Black Virgin hidden away in the shadows of the world. It was then that I began to recognise the sacred feminine within my own psyche.

Returning home, I experienced a need to begin an inner journey. I became a cave dweller as I learned what it meant to come into relationship with my inner truth. The time spent in the darkness of my cave was a necessary part of my becoming whole, and I began to study psychologies of the soul as a way of making meaning of my own life story.

In 2011, twenty-two years after my first visit, I was called by a dream to return to France and visit the place where my soul-awakening experiences began. Again, I travelled to a land of mystery, to a place I have always loved. France seemed to resonate with my sense of beauty, and there I found myself able to relax into the feminine parts of myself.

I had met the presence of the sacred feminine and felt her energy touch me. Slowly, my perceptions of my self changed, and my experiences began to create a new awareness of the essence of the feminine. I developed a deep connection with the authentic truth and beauty within me as a reflection of my soul and eventually, the archetype of the Creatress revealed herself to me.

I returned home to New Zealand and began to tell others I was writing a book. It was not until 2013 that I started to write my story - finding my voice as an older woman who has taken a long journey to heal herself and to manifest her feminine creative powers.

One morning, when I first began writing, I awoke suddenly: the word "creatrix" flashed into my mind as my very first thought of the day. Asking myself whether it was a real word, I rushed to look it up in my mother's treasured dictionary. There I found two words, both pregnant with meaning:

> Creatrix, defined as the feminine version of Creator
> - supreme being; one who creates.
> Creatress, described as she who has the power
> to create; a maker.

From this point of view, I began to glimpse the bigger picture of the feminine principle and to understand its importance in reclaiming my sense of soul, both personally and collectively.

∽

My story is unashamedly about the feminine as a primary creative principle that exists in the lives of men and women.

From an outer journey to an inner journey and beyond, my quest has become a transformational heroine's journey. As a woman in need of healing my heart, I opened to a deep connection with a personally felt sense of my soul: an ancient yet very new essence that lives at the heart of all matter.

∽

I write this story from my soul in the hope that it will touch your soul and inspire you to awaken to the unique sparkle of your truth:

> To follow your heart, to hear the voices of your soul,
> to love the feminine within.

Sometimes when I think I am going somewhere, life has a way of taking me along another path into experiences I could not have dreamed or imagined.

PART I

MY STORY: AN OUTER JOURNEY

1

TAKING A LEAP

It is 1989, the year of the Saturn-Neptune conjunction in Capricorn, a time when life is changing in surprising ways as the world of mystery and invisible realms meets with the world of boundaries and manifestations of physical forms. This is the year of the Tiananmen Square protests and the fall of the Berlin wall, as structures that have been supporting us begin to be tested. It is a time when the subtle realms of our existence are seeking to arise into consciousness in new ways, taking us beyond the limits of Saturn, to meet the realms of Neptune.

∽

It is a morning in late March. There is a slight coolness in the air. The sun is still brilliant on the leaves of the trees outside my bedroom window, but a promise that storms will soon be on their way hangs silently in the air. The best of this New Zealand summer is fading.

I am now forty and I feel an inner need for change. This morning I awoke to realise that I had come to a decision while I slept. Feelings came to me in the form of a deep knowing that if I do not change my life, something inside of me would die, never to be born again. I feel a driving urgency to take a risk, make a change, and follow the voice that had spoken to me in my dreams. The decision lies there in front of me, clear as clear could be.

TURNING my gaze into the future to see what I could imagine, I know I am about to begin a journey to the other side of the world in search of a sense of home. A journey that will become a voyage of learning and discovery, as the pieces of my experiences come together and align like the points of a perfect triangle. Something in me knows that they will.

Over breakfast, I talk with my children of my desire to take a trip to Europe and I suggest how great it would be for them to spend some time living with their father. The wheels of motion have been set into action: I have made a commitment to myself and there will be no turning back, no time to hesitate or to question my decision.

SATURDAY MORNING HAS ARRIVED and my children are visiting their father. I am alone and I notice a leaflet that has been lying on my table for days about a Gaia conference. I read it for the first time to find that it is starting in half an hour at the University of Auckland's School of Architecture. Having nothing planned for the day, I make an instant decision to go. I arrive to find an eclectic gathering of conservationists, scientists, astrologers, psychologists, and many others. The diverse group of people is so inspiring; it feels like stepping into an alternative reality. Over the course of the day, I meet an astrologer who tells me of astrological summer schools in London and I make a new friend in Suzanne, a woman who happens to sit next to me in a break and happens to choose the same lectures to go to. By the end of the day, we are making plans to meet again. Suzanne lives in London and offers to help me find accommodation there.

SYNCHRONICITIES ARE HAPPENING and my plans are quickly taking shape. And so, like the Fool in the tarot, I leave my home and family and venture out on a journey of 25,000 miles, taking just one step in front of the other with an open heart and a willingness to be led wherever I need to go.

ON THE WAY TO LONDON, I decide to stop over in San Francisco. I hope to meet Mary Greer, a marvellous writer of tarot books, who will be holding a workshop at a full moon women's gathering. After catching three Greyhound buses, I arrive on a farm, nestled in the mountainous foothills of the Sierra Nevada. This is a farm where they make flower essences and here is a gathering of creative and spiritually aware women. I feel grateful to be part of it all and to see Mary working with the Tarot.

Sitting in a circle, we each draw a card to represent ourselves. I draw the Star card, with the image of a naked woman pouring water into a river with the stars above her. This image expresses the energy of Aquarius so well, and resonates with my need to live my truth and to shine the light of my cosmic soul self in the world.

When my time at the farm is over, I decide to stay in a nearby town in Nevada for a few more days, and find a house in the village offering bed and breakfast.

One evening, I am invited to join a spiritual development circle run by a group of people learning to develop their psychic abilities. The room is quiet, and everyone focuses on the energy that is present. They place me in the centre of their circle, and tune into my energy. I feel the energy in the room, and I sense a strong and comforting presence beside me. Others in the group are amazed to perceive a very intense male energy in spirit standing beside me.

> *"I can see a male presence standing beside your right shoulder," the leader says. "He has a very strong light body and is standing very close to you. He tells me he is there to guide you on your journey. You have a long path ahead of you, and he will keep you safe and show you the way."*

As she speaks, his energy intensifies and I can feel his arms, not touching but around me; he is there to protect and guide me. Others in the group chime in with their own observations, saying how bright this spirit's light is shining.

> *"I have never seen a spirit that is so bright and strong and has so clear a presence,"* the leader affirms.

From that moment on, I have a greater awareness of the presence of my spirit guardian. I feel that I am protected as if there are angel wings wrapped around me and I am no longer alone on my journey. There would be many times that I would feel blessed by this presence and the help that so often came my way in the months ahead.

MY NEXT STOP IS LONDON, the place where my mother and father had met in 1944 at the time of the Second World War. She was working in the top-secret communication headquarters of the War Office in Whitehall—a network of secure underground bunkers where Churchill had his own rooms.

He was on leave in London from the Royal New Zealand Air Force where he was stationed on the west coast of Africa. Years ago, I had found my father's diary that described the moment when their lives crossed paths, the day they met at a tea dance. I walk in Green Park, gaze at the statue of Eros in Piccadilly Circus, and make a visit to Whitehall: all places where they would have gone together as they found themselves falling in love.

London was the place where the seeds of potential for my life were planted, and my mother's stories of her life there had made me believe it was my home too. After spending a month enjoying the vibe of London and going to a tarot workshop and lectures at Liz Greene's Centre for Psychological Astrology at Regent's Park, I find that I have some time to fill, before the astrology summer schools begin in August. I decide to spend a month travelling in France. France is a place I have always loved, ever since my first trip there when I was seventeen.

Taking the overnight fast train from London to Nice, I arrive at the Côte d'Azur the next morning. I book into a small room that is just big enough for the bed with my luggage squashed to the side and a bathroom the size of a cupboard. It is an oddly shaped two-star hotel, yet I feel so happy to be back in France.

Courage requires me to take a risk and follow the inner voice of my heart, putting just one step forward, followed by another as I journey into the unknown…..

2

INTUITION AND SYNCHRONICITY

AFTER SEVERAL DAYS EXPLORING NICE, I begin travelling westward on the train, not knowing where I am to spend the next night. When the train reaches Arles, I make the decision to disembark. The station has no taxis or info centre, so I head out towards the old town trundling my suitcase behind. I notice doves nestling in the alcoves of the old town's outer stonewalls as I enter through the archway in search of a hotel. After walking for quite a time, on a narrow, cobbled lane, I find the Hôtel Saint Trophime and book into a room.

RESTING on my bed this balmy summer's afternoon, I hear the most beautiful Mozart music wafting into my room from a pianist playing in the courtyard below. Tears well up in my eyes as the beauty and grace of the music touch my heart with its delicate harmonies, and I feel like I am in heaven. That evening I stroll through the old town and chose to dine in the Place du Forum under the flood-lit leafy trees.

ARLES IS one of those French towns, which carries the history of other cultures in its architecture. With an amphitheatre in the style of the Coliseum and a bullfighter's ring at the centre of the old town, it also has a number of art museums, one that was built in honour of Vincent van Gogh.

I spend the next day just walking through the narrow streets and taking photos. I notice that each door has its own distinct quality to it with particular colours and shapes, each so different from the next. I find the many shades of colours very beautiful, and they touch me emotionally with a subtle sensitivity that awakens my heart.

THE NEXT NIGHT, I return again to the Place du Forum. I take a table under the trees as the light of the day begins to fade and the magic of the night starts to fall. Everywhere restaurants spread their tables out from all directions, filling the cobbled square with tablecloths of many colours.

This is the month when the grand expose of photographers is in full swing. There are several large screens standing under the tall plane trees waiting to come alive with images when the light has changed to that illusionary time of darkness. The evening is all so very magical, and I feel happy with my decision to stay in Arles for five nights.

I meet a man this same night, an interesting man with an intelligent face who says he is here to find artwork for his gallery in Spain. Jacques plans to travel to the Camargue the next day with a group of friends, to see the gypsies and the wild white horses.

I would have loved to make this journey into the land of salt hills and rice fields and see the traditions of the gypsy peoples there, but something in me knows that I am not yet ready to leave the city of Arles.

Soon, I will travel further to the west, not to the south to visit Sainte-Marie-de-la-Mer, for I am feeling called by the mystery of Rennes le Chateau.

In the morning when I go down to breakfast, the hotel staff ask me when my room will be vacated. I am surprised to discover that I only have a booking for two nights!

A moment of panic arises in me: I am not ready to leave this town, and the two-hundredth-year celebration of Bastille Day is only two days away. What to do? After a moment, I hear a small voice within me say, *"pack your bags and just keep moving."* And so I do just that.

As I step out into the narrow, cobbled lane, taking a moment to decide which way to go, I begin walking and notice a woman also toting a suitcase coming towards me. I find myself walking along beside her and we begin to speak to each other. I ask where she is heading and discover she is making her way to a hotel overlooking the Arles Amphitheatre. I decide to tag along and see if there is a room available for me, knowing that this is very unlikely as this was high summer and it was festival time in Arles.

By the time we reach the top of the lane, she has offered to share her room of two single beds with me. What luck, and all in the space of a few minutes.

Now I have someone to spend Bastille Day with as well, for I had been warned not to venture out alone on that night: the French are known to let loose.

> It was when I arrived in Arles that I began to trust my inner voice and just take that next step, allowing myself to be led. I began to discover experiences of synchronicity, which were to become an everyday occurrence as I continued my travels.

OVER THE NEXT few days I get to know my new roommate Janine, who has lived a large part of her life as a nun and now lives with her partner in a Winnebago, travelling around the USA. We both enjoy spending time together, just sitting in cafés and watching the crowds go by instead of racing from place to place as if it were a contest to see how much could be viewed in a single day. We feel a natural affinity for each other as if we had been friends in another lifetime.

THE FOURTEENTH OF JULY—BASTILLE Day—rolls around, and the two-hundredth-year celebrations are about to begin. Janine and I decide to catch the train to Avignon for the day to see the parades. The flavours of French patriotism are on full display there, as parades of soldiers in colourful uniforms march through the streets. And the Pope's palace, we find, is an impressive monument to patriarchal power. This amazing day of celebrating French independence ends with us standing on the Pont d'Avignon watching the fireworks display.

The next day, saying goodbye on the train platform, we both fight back the tears as we hug and part. We are two like souls whose paths have crossed for only a few days, and we both feel a deep connection that we cannot explain.

MY NEXT STOP is the Languedoc (old Occitania).

As the train approaches Carcassonne, I can see the ancient double-walled castle in the distance and I decide to alight. I am intrigued by its magical, fairytale quality, with its ramparts, turrets, cobbled paths and stairways. It is a medieval city within a city. With the help of the info centre this time, I decide to stay within the castle walls and find a small hotel hidden away off one of the winding pathways.

THE ROOM IS old and filled with antique pieces, and the view from the window gives me a glimpse of the magical world I am about to explore. After settling into my room, I step out to wander through the cobbled streets lined with boutiques and cafés, and discover a small jewellery shop. As I browse the shelves, my eye catches a handcrafted silver pendant of a bird in flight attached to an equal-sided cross. The owner tells me that the piece is a symbol of the Cathar, a Gnostic religious order that had a strong presence in this part of France many centuries ago, before being persecuted by the Catholic Church.

I leave the shop wearing this silver Cathar symbol around my neck: a bird of freedom and the cross of matter.

> I have a sense that I am being guided and the clear,
> true voice of my intuition is becoming stronger.

Being alone, I know the only way to move forward is to trust myself and take the time to notice my feelings and the voice of insight that flashes through me. And to catch those flashes, I need to take notice whenever they come to me.

Could it be that I am opening a channel to the universal mind and to the voices of my feminine wisdom?

The words that come to me seem to be leading me in a synchronistic way to where I need to be, and the economy of their truth is becoming astounding.

∽

Nobody knows where I am, for I do not know myself where I will be each day, but I have a growing feeling of being led by a guiding hand.

My intuition grows stronger as I open myself to messages that arrive suddenly, messages which have a ring of truth about them that resonate with the whole of me.

3

BECOMING LOST

Today I set off to visit Quillan, the last stop on the local train line from Carcassonne in the direction of the Pyrénées mountains. I sit in the village square at a café watching the people around me, and decide not to stay the night here. Instead, I begin to retrace my steps and catch the train back to Couiza, the closest village to Rennes-le-Château. I have heard of the castle of the Duke of Joyeuse, and I like the idea of staying there. The train conductor flirts with me and suggests I meet him at the end of the day to go out for dinner—I doubt I'll take him up on the offer but I don't let him know that.

I can see the castle in the distance as I stand on the station platform, and I head in that direction pulling my suitcase along. The pathways of narrow, cobbled streets are full of twists and turns, and at one point it feels like the streets are closing in around me. It is becoming hard work to pull my trundler bag over the cobbles, and I have now lost sight of the castle. The heat of the noonday sun is making my journey slow, and I am beginning to feel I have made a mistake stopping here. Suddenly, I realise in dismay that I am lost.

I pause for a moment to drink from my water bottle and take in the situation. Just at that moment, a door opens in front of me and out tumbles a family who look at me in surprise. I begin to ask in French if they can tell me how to reach the castle, but the man smiles and answers in perfect English,

> "The castle is closed this time of year, so you will not be able to stay there. But if you would like to come with us, I can take you to a hotel that is owned by a friend of mine in a village nearby.
> I know you will like it there."

They seem to be a happy, friendly family, so without a moment's hesitation I trust this stranger as he lifts my suitcase into the boot of his car. Within minutes, we arrive at a small hotel in a village called Alet-les-Bains. He books me into a room and delivers my bag there too. I say my farewells to them all, and then they are gone. So this is how I find myself staying at the Hôtel l'Evêché in this small village close to Rennes-le-Château, without ever meaning to.

I settle myself into what is a large, dark room with a double bed. The double bed has a carved wooden bedhead, and the bathroom has a raised shower cubicle that looks like a space capsule. It is more spacious than I am used to, and a little quirky too. I feel so grateful and truly blessed to have this safe space to rest and relax in.

I throw open the window and lean out to see where I am, and find myself leaning over the river Aude as it flows against the stone walls of my hotel room. I can feel the freshness of the fast-moving water, and it seems to give me energy. I feel revived and I realise that my spirit guide has so elegantly looked after me yet again.

I HAD STEPPED out into a journey, not knowing where I was going or why, and I have arrived here in a small village beside a river. After the circuitous journey I have been on, I find this room and the sounds of the river comforting.

The next morning, I walk beside the river and find a place under the leafy trees. I sit down to ponder while surrounded by the sounds of the river Aude and the ancient ruins of a lost cathedral. I notice the old stones that lie in patterns on the ground. I sit on a low stone wall that echoes the river's path, and I have the feeling that these stones have stories to tell, of ancient times. This was Cathar country and their voices are still here in this land of spiritual energies. I feel very at home and I wonder, *could it be that I belonged to this place centuries before?*

THE SOUNDS and smells bathe me with their freshness and my breathing slows as I let go of my thoughts and a reverie overtakes me. I sit with nothing to do, nowhere to go, and I watch life flow all around me. I am still and I am open as my consciousness becomes at one with the river.

Life begins to slow around me; my heart slows too and all I can hear is the constant flow of this body of water drawing me in. I listen with an inner stillness, being present to this world that surrounds me. Pausing to ask myself why I am here in this small village in the Languedoc, tears threaten to emerge and feelings arise which overwhelm me with a familiar sadness.

As I sit here lost in these feelings, words force their way into my consciousness and I hear this answer arise as if the river speaks:

"*This is the story of a very lost soul.*"

My heart responds

"These words feel so very true to me."

Like a flash of lightning, I awaken into a new awareness. A realisation strikes me that these words are pregnant with meaning. This has been my truth and there is a beauty in this truth that speaks to my heart. Pieces, like dominos falling, are slotting onto each other and connecting me to a sense of that which has been missing, as I begin to make sense of my life.

A great sadness deepens within me and
I feel a heaviness I know so well.

Tears well up in my eyes and begin to roll slowly down my face and into my lap in large drops. I wipe them away with my hands. I feel so lost and alone sitting here, with my tears flowing in unison with the waters of the rushing river.

I had been a girl pretending to be a wife and a mother, not truly believing I deserved any of it. I had dreamed of a home and my own family and now it seemed that I had failed and my dream was now lost.

These feelings that came to me, they speak of something deep within my soul. Although they are very painful, they are also comforting as they reach into the very essence of my being, awakening me to the longings of my soul.

Eventually, the sounds of the river become louder and bring me back to the present. The freshness of the flowing river wakes me up with feelings of aliveness that the awareness of truth brings, and these words come to me:

> *Life is like a river, flowing on and on*
> *A great body of water that dances with its song*
> *We know not where we're going*
> *We know not from where we came and yet*
> *there is a passion that keeps stirring us along*
>
> *Everything is movement; at my centre is my song,*
> *It is what gives me meaning, the sighing of my soul.*
> *My rhythm and my dancing and my voice to sing along*
> *There is a passion at my centre flowing with my song*
> *Life is like a river flowing on and on.*

THE THOUGHT COMES to me that we each have our own music within us, our rhythm of life that vibrates with every cell of our being, making our unique resonance with the world around us. And with this moment begins my first initiation into hearing the voice of my soul. I have begun a journey that is leading me into my depths, and I am learning to listen and to ponder over messages that come from subtle ways of knowing and being.

I am beginning to connect to the flow of energy that is both personal and beyond personal, and I am able to rest here, for I have a feeling of coming home to this place that resonates so strongly with my soul.

Following my intuition, I have allowed myself to be pulled backwards into a time and place I thought was foreign to me. I have the feeling that I lived here long ago in an ancient time, and these stones have stories to tell of a time before the inquisitions when the messages of the

Cathar and Mary Magdalene resonated in this land, and the river sings her songs.

IN THE EVENING, I attend a talk on the Cathar. It is in French, and I don't understand much of what is said, but I see how passionately they speak of this other time in history. It is all a mystery to me, and yet it serves to make me aware of how alive the Cathar traditions are still in the Languedoc.

THE NEXT MORNING, I breakfast in the restaurant with its red-and-green tablecloths. The day is already beginning to warm up and lazy flies are circling the room, alighting on tabletops in search of some remnants of food. I wonder what the day will bring, and if I can find a way to get to Rennes-le-Château. It is the stories of unexplained treasure found there and the mystery of the place that has drawn me to the Languedoc, but without a car, there is no way to arrive.

It is only when I become lost that I am able to uncover my true path - the path that leads me home to my soul.

4

RENNES-LE-CHÂTEAU

I AM in Cathar country and the mysterious village of Rennes-le-Château is not far from here.

The passion and interest I observed last night when I attended a talk about the Cathar intrigued me and I am determined to find a way to visit Rennes-le-Château, although I know that without a car, to get there is impossible.

There, seated at another table having their breakfast, is a friendly English couple. I smile across to them and say hello. They tell me that they have just bought a holiday cottage and are waiting for the lawyer to finalise the papers for them to sign before they journey over the Pyrenees into Spain, to catch their plane home to England.

I describe to them how I heard talk of the mysteries of Rennes-le-Château when I was in London, and that this village is only a short drive from here. I share with them my curiosity about the mystery surrounding the place, that explains the reason I find myself staying in Alet-les-Bains.

They offer to drive me there, as they have some time to spare. They suggest I pack my bag and they will drop me off at another village close to Rennes-le-Château on their way to Spain.

SOON, we are in their small rental car heading up the mountainous road to explore this village of intrigue. As we travel up a winding gravel road, I relay to my companions the little I know of the stories of mystery at Rennes-le-Château. I recount that a priest named Bérenger Saunière had discovered a treasure here and how as a result of this, he had renovated the buildings in lavish style and he never disclosed the secret of how he had come by his wealth.

The buildings and landscape here are said to contain coded messages as well as references to Mary Magdalene, as she was thought to have lived here long ago.

By the time the road ends and we pull up in the dusty car park, we are excited and feel a shared sense of adventure.

Arriving at noon, we find the village is deep in midday slumber. Set on a hillside with views across the countryside in all directions, this small village appears to be deserted. There is no one to be seen anywhere.

We wander about until we reach the gardens of the Villa Bethania with the Tour Magdala beyond. From the belvedere walkway we can see way across to the hills and valleys of the Languedoc. The tower, which is said to have housed an extensive library of books, is locked so we wander back through the gardens until we arrive at the village church.

TO OUR SURPRISE, here in the hilltop village of Rennes-le-Château is a very unusual *église de Marie Madeleine*. Even before entering the church, I notice a sign over the doorway that says "terribilis est locus iste." At first, I think this means "this place is terrible," but I later discover that it means this place is truly awe-inspiring and one should look upon it with a respect akin to reverential wonder.

Upon entering, I am greeted by a statue of Asmodeus that looks like the devil. He is a horned and winged demon and he holds a stoup of holy water on his shoulders. Walking on, we enter into the darkness of the church and turn right to see down the aisle towards the altar. The first thing I notice is a bas-relief on the front of the altar of a woman sitting, holding a book, with a skull resting beside her. My first thought is, *this could be symbolic of Mary Magdalene's story*. On each side of the altar there are statues: one is the Virgin and Child and the other is Joseph and Child.

The statues in this church and the scenes in the windows are all intriguingly different. The statue of Saint Anthony of Padua is the largest of them all and stands holding a book and a child on a plinth supported by four angels. He is said to be helpful in finding lost things. The statue of Mary Magdalene has a skull, book, goblet, and staff, and stands between statues of Saint Roche, with a wound on his thigh and a dog beside him, and Saint Anthony of Padua. There are also two statues on the left of the aisle, which are Saint Germaine with two sheep, and Saint Anthony of Egypt with a staff, book, and pig. This church named after Mary Magdalene is unusual in its layout, as well as the statues it contains. It all feels strangely and unforgettably feminine to me.

∽

LATER, we find François Bérenger Saunière's grave in the church grounds, and on his tombstone we read the words:

Marie-Madeleine - L'énergie Divine Féminine
François Bérenger Saunière
11 April 1852 - 22 January 1917

BÉRENGER SAUNIÈRE WAS a man of mystery whose wish was to create a sanctuary in honour of Mary Magdalene that would rival the sanctuary at Lourdes. In his time as the village priest, he rebuilt Rennes-le-Château in extravagant style. It is believed that he became rich as a result of something he found while restoring the crypt of this village church. Therein lies the mystery, for he only revealed the truth of what he found to his housekeeper. She died sometime after him, but she never revealed his secret. And although the village has been destroyed at times, this church has always remained unscathed.

The pope investigated Bérenger Saunière and could find no explanation for his wealth and power. Some suggest that Marie, a princess of Pays de Sault who died in 1781, had left ancient family documents and personal treasures with her priest, Antoine Bigou, who hid them in the church at Rennes-le-Château. These documents may have related to the writings of Mary Magdalene and the Cathar of ancient times.

I FIND that this place is rich with symbols of feminine energy. The number twenty-two, for instance, is seen in some important dates: 22 July is Mary Magdalene's feast day and Bérenger Saunière died on 22 January. He constructed the Tour Magdala with twenty-two steps leading to the top and twenty-two battlements at the top, linking it to the garden below with twenty-two steps. The skull at the entrance of the gravesite has twenty-two teeth and the inscription found over the door of the church—"terribilis est locus iste"—has twenty-two letters. The number twenty-two is a powerful, spiritual number of the master teacher, who has unique talents for manifesting ideas into the realm of reality.

Feminine energy is also reflected by the geography of the place: the pentacle, a five-pointed star, is mapped out in the land by mountaintops around Rennes-le-Château. The five-pointed star is also the pattern made by the transit of the planet Venus as it completes a full eight-year cycle, and as such, is a symbol of love and feminine powers.

The presence of Mary Magdalene is another potent symbol of feminine energy. Here in this church, Mary Magdalene is shown in the name, in the image on the altar and her statue, and again in the words on Bérenger Saunière's tombstone. I believe that when something occurs three times over it becomes a theme for that person or place.

OUR TIME IS short and I have the feeling I will visit this place again; there is something here that intrigues me even though we leave having spoken to no one. My curiosity is stirred and I depart with many unanswered questions and much to ponder.

Not knowing is part of life, for it makes space for the hidden mysteries and allows us to awaken to the sacredness of the feminine way.

5

QUILLAN AT THE FULL MOON

I AM BACK in Quillan again, the last stop on the train line. It is here that Cherie and Michael dropped me off on their way to their lawyer's office and then to Barcelona airport.

JUST THE DAY BEFORE, while I was sitting by the river Aude in Alet-les-Bains, I felt the deep sadness of my soul. Little did I know that everything was about to change: this is the night of the full moon when her powerful magnetic energy is in full force.

I FIND a small room in the hotel at the crossroads just as we enter Quillan and I am shown to a corner room that has a single bed with a window on the opposite wall. I have decided to rest a little after my day's adventures, and so I lie on my narrow bed with the window fully open and listen to the sounds of families out strolling on this balmy summer evening.

Slowly, the moon begins to rise and fill my window with its silvery light. Soon, I find that I am bathed in moonlight from my toes to the top of my head.

The moon appears large and fills my window frame with its shining light. I can feel its energy flowing over me.

After some time, I begin to feel a shift as the moon's energy starts to move in waves right through me. The light of the moon is caressing me, washing all of me with her gentle, easy flow of magnetic energy. It feels like waves surging through me, bathing me with the purest energy, washing through the core of my being. The moonlight feels as if it is gently and strongly realigning my chromosomes and all the cells of my body in tune with its magnetic feminine force. I begin to relax deeply, and slip off into a meditative state. After some time I awaken from this loving lunar presence. A sense of completion descends upon me, and I feel happy and full of energy.

This evening, I decide to treat myself to a full meal rather than the cup of soup or noodles I often take in my room at night. I cross the road to the restaurant opposite the hotel, and sit on the patio surrounded by groups of people out enjoying themselves. There is a feeling of happiness in the air matching my inner experience. After a wonderful meal, I return to my room and soon drift off into a peaceful sleep.

The next morning, I awake knowing that I have experienced something subtle, powerful and life changing. I have a knowing that it is now time to turn around and retrace my steps and begin the long journey home to New Zealand.

In a small space of time, from the moment I was lost in search of the castle of the Duke of Joyeuse, I have been chauffeured to three different places, each of which has had a profound influence on how I experience my world.

I have been touched by the grace of the moon. The cells of my body have been rearranged by the magnetic waves of the moon's energy, and I feel deeply changed and re-aligned by this feminine energy. I now know what it means to be bathed by the light of the moon: a gentle, loving softness that makes me feel blessed. I find myself thinking that being at this place, in this moment of time, was my destiny.

THIS HAS BECOME a time that marks a turning point in my life. My choices from this time onwards will be filtered through my awakened awareness of sacred presence of the feminine.

I will pay a price for this change, for I can no longer follow the path of external focus but must now follow the path of inner knowing. Although I did not know it at this time, the feminine in me was beginning to heal.

I have been drawn to the mystery and magic of Rennes-le-Château and over this period of three days, I heard the voice of my soul; visited a place where the mystery of the sacred feminine and Mary Magdalene is honoured; and experienced a healing by the light of the moon.

Blessed by the moon's light, I have a deep knowing that this journey is now complete.

The full moon showed her power to me, cleansing and healing every cell of my body with her magnetic light, activating the wise woman within me.

6

RETURNING HOME

AFTER A SHORT STOP in Limoux and then Carcassonne, I take the long train ride following the Mediterranean coastline back to Nice. I have been told of a small town just a short train ride from Nice, so I head off in the direction of Italy and within minutes I arrive at Villefranche-sur-Mer.

I AM GREETED by masses of purple bougainvillea flowering all along the cliff edge of the train station, making a divide between me, and the glistening waters of the Mediterranean sea. The village is set on a steep hillside with a curved deepwater harbour. There are remnants of ancient Roman influences to be found in the narrow, tunnelled roadways, and restaurant tables that appear in the evenings make the pathways even narrower. There are houses of pink and yellow, red and purple, and flowers hang everywhere.

Just beside the village of Villefranche-sur-Mer is a peninsula of land called Saint-Jean-Cap-Ferrat, where author Daphne du Maurier and the Rothschild banking family have lived.

THE NEXT DAY, I walk along the shoreline to where Saint-Jean-Cap-Ferrat begins, and find there is a bus going to the village at the end of the peninsula. I climb aboard and soon arrive at the town. I follow a winding path, which leads to the tip of the peninsula. At the end of the path I reach a church, and there I find an amazing sight: beside the church, standing almost as tall as the steeple, is a bronze statue of a woman holding a child. She and her child are wearing a crown and in her other hand she holds a sceptre. I take her photo, noticing that my shoulder sack and sun hat are the same size as the sandalled foot that they rest against.

I HAVE JUST MET my first *Vierge Noire* statue. This particular sculpture is a modern-day statue built by a wealthy man as an expression of his thanks for her healing blessings.

While waiting for the bus, I meet a local woman and I show her a postcard image I had bought of the statue. Her face lights up and she lets me know how blessed and loved she feels by this Madonna with her gesticulations and her words and signs of prayer. Again, I find myself intrigued by a powerful presence of the feminine here in France.

MY TIME in France is now over, and I return to England where I immerse myself in astrology again with a weeklong summer school at Jesus College, Oxford, and more lectures at Regent's College in London. I am learning from astrologers such as Dr Liz Greene and Howard Sasportas who are also psychologists, and they are changing my thinking as well as the way that I interpret the world around me.

At one of the lectures, I am invited to attend a five-day workshop to be held at the Wrekin Trust in the Malvern Hills. Without a moment's hesitation, I agree to go. There I meet Howard Sasportas, the author of books I have read such as *The Gods of Change* and *The Twelve Houses*. It is Howard who introduces me to the ancient Greek myth of Psyche and describes the lessons contained in her soul journey.

After five wonderful days immersed in astrology, I leave feeling so honoured to have spent this time with him. Before I go, Howard tells me that I have the answers to anything I need to know already within me.

Is he referring to my intuition or the feminine ways of knowing, which are growing stronger within me, or my connection to higher wisdom? His words have stayed with me forever.

I HAVE SO ENJOYED the active community of psychological astrologers, but my family is calling me so I reluctantly book my flight home. I leave the mysteries of France and the inspiration of London, and travel back through the USA to my home in New Zealand. Arriving home, my outer journey has come to an end, but I bring with me new experiences and many unanswered questions. The task of meaning making has already begun: I had listened to the voice that called me to begin my travels, I had taken risks and allowed myself to be guided along the way, and now there can be no going back to my former life as an unawakened soul.

BACK AT HOME, I am in that uncomfortable place where I feel changed but everything around me seems the same as before. Beginnings and endings can be confusing times: I am no longer the person I was, and I have not yet fully embodied the person I am now becoming. I cannot go back to being the old me, and I have no clear vision of who the new me is. The rules I have lived by no longer serve me, and so I begin the process of sifting and sorting through my perceptions to find, that which resonates with me now. The changes are non-negotiable, and I am in the most uncomfortable state of transition between being lost and being found as my authentic soul-self arises within me.

MY INTUITION, however, has grown stronger, and I hear my inner voice singing to me. Whenever I ignore her messages, I am reminded that my inner wisdom speaks with the voice of my truth. I now find that when I speak a truth to another person, I feel a flow of energy rush down my spine as if to say *"yes, this is true,"* and when I hesitate in my speech, a little voice inside me says, "don't say that," or "take your time," or "step back for a moment," which I ignore at my peril.

I am also growing more aware of subtle energies all around me, and find myself reading the energy of the moment.
If I quieten my mind and breathe into an awareness of each moment, I discover that I have the freedom to respond sensitively to what is present at the time.
I find I am less fearful of what life brings, and can live in the flow of life, as if in tune with the river that spoke to me.
I feel more trusting and spontaneous in my responses to the world, and allow creative forces to reveal themselves to me.
I notice synchronicities as they occur around me, guiding

me in magical ways. As my sense of the feminine within me grows, so too does the voice of my soul.

I FEEL invisible to those around me as I re-enter a place where I no longer feel I belong. I need to take time to reflect on my journey, so that I can begin to find the words to describe all that I have experienced in France.

This need draws me into an exploration of myth and psychology as a way to understand myself and expand my consciousness. Just like that, another path opens, I now journey without a map to guide me.

My first sight of La Vierge Noire, the tall statue of mother and child towering above the church steeple, feels important in ways I don't yet understand.

PART II

HER STORY: A HEROINE'S JOURNEY

7

THE MYTH OF PSYCHE

As I take the long flights back to my homeland, I have the feeling that I am going to the very end of the earth and away from all that has fascinated and fed me. And in a way, I am. But on my return home, I begin the search for ways to make meaning of my experiences.

I ponder my journey and I begin to realise that I am on a heroine's quest to know my feminine soul. In my search for meaning making on this heroine's journey, I look to the myth of Psyche; an archetypal feminine story that leads Psyche from innocence to maturity and feminine empowerment.

There are similarities between the hero and the heroine's quests, as they both must journey alone into the unknown, letting go of all that they have relied upon. They both must take a risk and learn to trust in themselves. But differences can be found in the lessons they must learn, the territory they must enter, and how they go about finding that which they seek. The hero quests outwardly, searching for the Holy

Grail as something to be found outside of himself. The elements of a hero's path are different and I leave his story for another time.

The heroine's quest, by contrast, is one of inward discovery: to find the Holy Grail that exists inside of herself.

As for the mythic tale of Psyche, there are many versions, each with subtle differences. The ancient Greeks were storytellers before the advent of paper, and so there is some variation according to oral tradition.

THE MYTH OF PSYCHE, as it was told to me, proceeds thus:

> *Psyche was born the third daughter of a king and queen. As she grew, she became beautiful beyond compare, even more beautiful than the goddess Aphrodite herself. Psyche had both inner and outer beauty, the shining beauty of her soul radiated from her, and people began to worship her as if she was a goddess. She was so luminous and pure that no man came forth to ask for her hand in marriage.*
>
> *Aphrodite, the goddess of love, heard that Psyche was being worshipped for her grace and beauty, as if she were a goddess, and she noticed that people were no longer worshipping at her own temple. This brought forth her wrath, and she became jealous of Psyche. Aphrodite decided to cast a spell so that Psyche would fall in love with the first man or monster she sees, and sent her son Eros to do the deed. But when Eros arrived to cast the spell on Psyche, he slipped and wounded himself with the arrow that was meant for her. He had spiked himself instead, and fell deeply in love with Psyche.*
>
> *Meanwhile, since no man had yet come forth to marry Psyche, her father asked an oracle for advice. As Psyche's father knew, when you ask the oracle a question, you are bound by the answer. The oracle replied to him,*

"The virgin is destined to be the bride of no mortal lover. Her future husband awaits her on the top of the mountain, and he is one whom neither gods nor men can resist."

Psyche, in her innocence is dressed for this ceremony and taken to the mountaintop where she was left alone to be sacrificed to her unknown fate. For her, there was a loss of home, family, and all that she knew. Psyche felt she was being punished for her beauty, and her life seemed doomed to sadness.

However, at that moment, Aphrodite's son Eros spied the beautiful maiden he had fallen in love with, and sent Zephyr, the west wind, to waft her down to the valley below. Eros came to her rescue, and she was magically transported into a romantic world where she lived in a beautiful castle and she began her relationship with this mysterious lover.

The implicit agreement was that she would live in this beautiful castle and Eros would visit her every night and shower love and passion upon her. He would, however, be gone every morning. He told her that if she tried to see him in the light of day, the spell would be broken.

So their secret life began, with Aphrodite, Psyche's mother-in-law, having no knowledge of it.

The magical castle carried the illusion of perfection, but this happiness was not destined to last. In time, Psyche's sisters came to visit, even though Eros had warned her against it. They became jealous of Psyche's seemingly luxurious existence and asked Psyche questions about her life that she could not answer. They began to cast seeds of doubt in Psyche's mind, and plotted a scheme to uncover the truth of who her lover really was.

When they left, their words played on Psyche's mind. The sister's urgings to see who he really was and her own curiosity got the better of her, so she decided to follow their cunning plan. She hid a dagger and a lamp close by her bed, and that evening she came to her lover while he slept.

With a dagger in one hand and a lamp in the other, she leaned over her sleeping lover to see for the first time the truth of who he really was. She was prepared to kill him should he be the monster her sisters suggested. She held up the lamp and there, lying before her, was the most wonderful sight: a man more beautiful than she had ever seen, with the wings of a god. She recognised her husband to be the god Eros, and she instantly fell even more deeply in love with him. He was so handsome, and his wings told the truth of his identity as a God. As she leaned over him to see his face more clearly, inadvertently a drop of the oil from her lamp spill onto his shoulder.

Awaking to see her with the lamp and dagger in hand, Eros was instantly angered. Their pact was now broken. He spread his wings and flew out of her life, leaving her all alone. The magic castle she called home vanished too, and she found herself standing in a meadow. Psyche (soul) and Eros (love) were now estranged from each other.

Psyche found herself left to wander alone. She discovered she was pregnant and was thrown into a state of despair, grieving the loss of her beloved. All she could do was to surrender to her situation. With this loss of her beloved, she entered a transition zone and the story of her transformation was about to begin.

Psyche started to wander the world in search of Eros. She felt that all was lost and there was no hope for her: not only had she lost her lover, but she knew she was carrying Eros' child in her womb. A child who would have been born immortal had she not broken their pact. Now, her child would be a mortal being.

She tried to end her life by throwing herself into the roaring river, but the river threw her back to the safety of the land.

The river said to her,
"Don't give up. There is much ahead for you, so take heart. You must surrender to what is, and not give up hope. Listen and learn to flow like the river, and keep moving onwards."

With a determination to be reunited with her lover, she set out alone. There would be no handsome prince to rescue her from the challenges that lay before her. She wandered aimlessly for some time, and nobody was able to help her. After a time, she went to speak with Aphrodite to plead for her help to become reunited with Eros.
Aphrodite was very displeased to discover that Psyche, a mere mortal, was her son's lover. She was not happy and she decided to set a challenge for Psyche. Being a cunning goddess, she set one task after the other, believing them to be way beyond Psyche's abilities. Her desire was to block Psyche from ever being reunited with her son Eros.

The four tasks that Aphrodite set for Psyche were each more difficult than the last, and each with its own lesson. Despite her great sadness, Psyche was willing to do whatever was asked of her on the journey ahead.
The first task she was given was that of sorting seeds. She was placed in a room with a mountain of seeds at the centre, and was asked to sort each kind of seed into separate piles by the morning. Overwhelmed with the task ahead, Psyche felt despair descend upon her. Just at that moment, an army of ants appeared, each taking one seed at a time, working all night until every seed was sorted.
She saw how the ants were able to take the time to discriminate between each separate seed, and place it where it belonged. The task was long and slow, but the results were impressive.

The next morning, Aphrodite was amazed to discover that the task had been completed. Psyche, feeling relieved and expecting to now be reunited with her lover, was dismayed to find that Aphrodite set another task to challenge her.

This time, the task was to gather the golden fleece from the rams that live in the Elysian fields. Psyche went to see the rams. They were powerful and actively competitive, playing games, butting heads, and fighting in the noonday sun. Psyche feared that she would be trampled to death by these rams if she tried to gather some of their golden fleece. Again, she felt the task was too great for her to complete, and so she stepped back to ponder what to do. Just then, she heard a voice coming from the reeds by the river. It said,

"Bide your time, as when the sun sets the rams will take their rest and then you will be able to enter their field and gather fleece from the bushes and fences."

Following the voice, Psyche waited until the sun became low in the sky and the rams were slowing into a drowsy state. Only then did she go about her task of collecting the golden fleece. Gathering all she needed, she withdrew to the safety of the riverbank.

Again, Aphrodite was surprised to see that Psyche has gathered the golden fleece. Maybe she had underestimated the young woman. So this time Aphrodite set another task, requiring a degree of delicacy and precision that was sure to be beyond the skills of Psyche. The task was to fill a crystal flask with pure water from the source of the river Styx.

Psyche followed the river to the source where a waterfall flowed into the river. She set out to climb the rocky face and reach the top of the waterfall, but the way up was steep and slippery and she feared for her life. As she bravely made her way up the craggy mountainside, an eagle saw her plight and swooped down to offer his services. Taking the crystal chalice in his talons, he flew to the top of the waterfall and filled it with the purest water. He returned it to Psyche without spilling a drop. Grateful, she carefully carried the precious water to Aphrodite and asked once again to be reunited with Eros. But again, her request was without success.

Aphrodite was now ready to charge Psyche with the most dangerous task of all: that of venturing into the underworld to visit Persephone, the queen of the underworld, and fetching some of Persephone's beauty potion. Psyche was to bring the potion back to Aphrodite, unopened.

Psyche knew that to enter the underworld meant to die, and so she climbed to the top of a tower to throw herself off. But the voice of the tower called to her,

"There is another way. I will show you how."

Psyche was told what she must do to enter the underworld and return safely. She was given two coins to pay the ferryman to cross the river Styx, and two cakes to feed the three-headed dog that guards the entrance. She was warned that along the way, she would be tested three times and she would need to say "no" three times and she was given a final warning not to open the box of beauty potion, for it was only for Aphrodite.

Following these instructions, Psyche paid the ferryman and fed the three-headed dog guarding the entrance. Entering the darkness of the underworld, she met with a man who pleaded with her to help him, and she remembered to say no and stay focused on her task. She needed both hands to safely hold the beauty box and could not afford to be distracted from her task. Twice again, she was asked to give help and twice again she said no. Gradually, she sensed her way through this unknown realm and met with Persephone, the queen of the underworld. Persephone gave Psyche the precious gift of the beauty potion for Aphrodite, and Psyche began to retrace her steps. After feeding the dog and paying the ferryman again, she arrived back in her familiar world with the treasured box.

By this time, she was very tired and thought to herself that if

she could just have a little of the beauty potion, she would look beautiful when she was at last reunited with her lover.
Psyche opened the box. Inside was a powder that put her into a deep sleep. Just as she was about to reach the end of her journey, she slipped up and so there she lay motionless, in a slumber, looking like a sleeping beauty.
Just at this time, Eros happened to be flying past and spied his beloved lying on the path below him. He had been missing her greatly, and he flew to her side directly. With his godly powers, he broke the spell of the sleeping potion by gathering it up, and putting it back into the box. Psyche awoke to see him, and together they went to give Persephone's gift to Aphrodite. Aphrodite had begun to see how much they loved each other, and began to accept Psyche. So Eros flew to Mount Olympus to ask the gods' permission for Psyche to be made immortal, and they agreed. She was offered a cup of ambrosia, which she drank and thus became a goddess. In time, a baby girl was born to them, and her name was Joy.

From here on, the story is one of lovers reunited, but this time it is with both eyes wide open. A conscious relationship of matured masculine and awakened feminine, for they have both grown from their experiences of loss and challenge. Eros and Psyche are now together, as love (Eros) is united with soul (Psyche) in a true marriage of trust. A child named Joy is the creative outcome of their coming together. There is a celebration, a sharing of their Joy with others, for it is no longer a secret relationship.

This myth of Psyche is a story of feminine magic that holds the power to open us to our own soul story.

8

PSYCHE'S TASKS

Let's take a closer look into the myth of Psyche to understand the heroine's lessons contained within her tale. The four tasks presented to Psyche have been designed by Aphrodite with the intention that Psyche, a mere mortal, would fail them all. There is value in exploring each of these tasks, as they carry symbolic meanings and important lessons to be learned from each of these experiences.

> Task One: To sort a mountain of seeds.
> Task Two: To gather the golden fleece from the solar rams.
> Task Three: To collect a chalice of the purest water from the source of the river Styx.
> Task Four: To enter the underworld and return with a box of beauty potion from the queen of the underworld.

The first task is to sort a huge pile of seeds. The ants do the sifting and sorting, focusing on the details and deciding which goes where, taking many small steps that each add up to the task being completed.

The ants are symbolic of the ability to work hard and to sift and sort through the minutia of life. It is a detailed and laborious task that needs to be done at the start of any new cycle. This involves the need to make decisions and to discriminate between what to keep and what to let go of, and to sort the seeds of possibility. Psyche learns the art of discrimination.

THE SECOND TASK is to collect some of the golden fleece from the solar rams. These rams are dangerous and Psyche risks being trampled by them. With the reeds' help, Psyche learns to have patience, to take her time, to use stealth, choosing carefully how and when to act. She learns how to approach a situation indirectly rather than head on, for the solar rams are big, strong, and dangerous. She also learns to honour her own rhythms and to listen to the voice of the reeds as they guide her. The reeds are organic and grow out of the waters of the river. They are connected to the natural flow of life. Psyche learns the lessons of strategy, timing, and developing trust in one's inner rhythms.

THE THIRD TASK is to collect pure water in a crystal flask from the top of the waterfall at the source of the river Styx. An eagle comes to her aid, taking hold of the goblet and flying to the source to gather the pure water. These waters represent the flow of life and cycles of creativity. Psyche is asked to gather some of this fluidity, and give it containment.

The eagle is symbolic of the ability to see the overall picture, to go beyond the immediate situation, to be able to see what is needed while at the same time staying focused, keeping one's eye on the task at hand. Psyche learns the lesson of seeing from another perspective—an eagle-eye view. Seeing the bigger picture makes it possible for her to uncover new and creative solutions.

After completing the first three tasks, Psyche is faced with the ultimate test. The next lessons she encounters do not come naturally to her. To survive this journey, she needs to make new choices and find ways to stay open and guided.

THE FOURTH TASK is for Psyche to travel into the underworld and to return with a box of beauty potion from Persephone, the queen of the underworld. This task is challenging and there are rules that are foreign to her, which she must learn in order to navigate the darkness of the underworld.

This is the advice she receives:

- To set her intention, to stay focused, and to not look back.
- To refrain from talking to anyone on the way, or becoming diverted by the plight of others.
- To take two coins to pay the ferryman each time she crosses the river Styx. She must be willing to pay the price when needed.
- To take two cakes to feed the three-headed dog, to distract them from guarding the entrance. On entering, and again on leaving the Underworld.
- To collect the box of beauty potion and to return without opening the box.

Psyche makes all the right choices as she moves through this dark realm. She is just about to complete her task of all tasks and it is then that she falters. Luckily, Eros who comes to her rescue at last. Psyche not only survives her experience in the underworld, she has returned with something precious and is finally reunited with her lover.

∽

Each of the four tasks become experiences for Psyche to grow as she learns new ways and gains a sense of achievement. Her path leads from despair, to darkness, to achievement, and through these experiences she matures as a woman in touch with her feminine essence. Eros, too, has grown from the experience of his separation from Psyche.

As she sensed her way through the darkness of the unknown, Psyche had to be willing to let go of that which no longer served her, and trust her inner guidance. She had to keep moving in search of the god of love (Eros), for it is love that awakens us to the truth that lives within our soul (Psyche).

Aphrodite's judgment of Psyche changes when she sees that Psyche has met all the challenges and grown in her power as a woman. She can see how much they love each other, and she gives them her blessing. Finally, Psyche is reunited with Eros in a conscious relationship of equals and she is made a goddess. Now immortal, she marries Eros and they begin a conscious relationship of two mature souls with the blessing of Aphrodite.

∽

The story is essentially a solo journey where Psyche learns to listen to the guidance from the world around her and strengthens her connection to her own inner wisdom and authority. Her story is the heroine's archetypal journey of transformation from innocence to empowerment; as she matures into owning the immortal part of herself ~ her soul.

As Psyche moves through her transformational journey, she matures in ways that can be related to different goddesses.

> Throughout the story, she progresses from -
> A maiden/Kore; a lover/Aphrodite;
> a pregnant woman and mother/Demeter;
> a bride/Hera; an immortal goddess/Psyche.

> She has also embodied Hestia—the inner flame of her truth at her sacred centre; and is guided by Hecate—a wise woman who helps her to navigate the crossroads.

Finally, Psyche bears a divine child named Joy - the creative child that represents Psyche's innocence, the awakening of her inner child-self, and her ability to live creatively and with spontaneity and a love of life. Joy represents Psyche's ability to trust in the creative process as it unfolds before her.

> In this story it is Aphrodite, the goddess of love, who sets the scene for Psyche's tale to unfold and initiates her path to maturity, individuation, and soul.

Psyche's story resonates with my own transformational experiences, and it becomes a comforting guide on this seemingly lonely path. This path that I must follow took me into the darkness of the underworld, where I entered the hidden places within me. It was in this darkness that instincts became my guide, and other subtle ways of knowing resurfaced into my consciousness. To go into the underworld is to enter a place of shadows and hidden mysteries, where everything familiar is gone. In this place of darkness and transition, I learned to trust in myself and to know the truth that lives in my heart.

ON MY RETURN from my travels, I entered a place of depth and mystery. I knew something had deeply changed within me, and I could not re-enter the old world of my immaturity. I began to look more closely at the nuances of Psyche's story as it related to me, and I realised that we cannot skip the steps on her journey or speed up the process of this archetypal heroine's path. This path of transformation is open to us all, but it takes its own course in its own time.

Psyche's lessons are all about trust, taking her beyond her rational logos mind into a feminine way of knowing: Gnosis

NUANCES OF A HEROINE'S JOURNEY

"Psyche" is the Greek word for Soul ~

WHICH IS something we may consider to be outside of ourselves. However, it can be found within us and is our personally felt sense of soul. It is in the telling of Psyche's tale that the essence of the heroine's journey unfolds.

THERE ARE SO many nuances to the essential nature of Psyche's story. Beginning with a willingness to take a risk. Like the Fool in the tarot, a heroine must leave the comfort of the known behind and travel alone and have the courage to step into the unknown with a beginner's mind, and surrender to the path as it unfolds before her over time.

IN THE HEROINE'S STORY, it is often the experience of loss that motivates her to step out on her journey. Psyche is led towards tests that become her transformational path.

The lessons she learns along the way expand her awareness of her inner feminine wisdom, and guide her to own her strength as a confidant and empowered woman.

The four tasks set to challenge her, are found in many of our transformational experiences and hold lessons for us all. Psyche is within everyone; she is our personal soul self.

HOWARD SASPORTAS in a lecture on Psyche in August 1989, said

> *"these four tasks are symbolic of the vital lessons we need to learn to transform from innocent maiden and become a mature, empowered, feminine queen."*

Psyche found herself alone on her path and in her despair she opens to guidance from the world around her. There are many sources of help that come to her in the form of her connection to plants, insects, birds, voices of the river, and the tower. They each appeared as her teachers, guides and helpers with lessons to teach her -

- The ants - perseverance, hard work and discrimination.
- The reeds - how to proceed in flow with life itself.
- The solar rams - Take her time and proceed with strategy when entering the masculine world of competition and physical prowess.
- The eagle - the ability to expand her perspective and to see a bigger picture.
- The tower - stay true to herself and owning her worth.

Every one of these characters in Psyche's tale are symbolic, and these symbols contain layers upon layers of meaning. They also represent the more subtle, psychological qualities that Psyche begins to develop with the power to connect us to our own soul story.

THE LIFE-GIVING waters of **the river Styx** is the border to the underworld and flows from the source where Psyche must collect the goblet of pure water. Water is the element associated with emotions, and being able to move in the creative flow attuned to the essence of life itself.

The crystal goblet represents being able to contain water ~ that which is symbolically fragile, by capturing creative energies, visions, and emotions, and giving them shape and form through containment.

The underworld is about learning how to go into a world of darkness and mystery. Psyche has to trust in her instincts and intuition in order to face the possibility of death and return alive with the gift of something precious.

The magical castle where all of Psyche's needs are met by invisible hands represents a world of illusion based upon a romantic dream of perfection that does is not real.

Finally, **Psyche's pregnancy** is symbolic of the transformational journey itself. She is endowed with the potentiality of the birth of her true, empowered, authentic self. Her pregnancy is also a symbol of the potential birth of the sacred self as soul — the divine child within us all. Psyche is transformed through her inner journey into a beautiful butterfly (soul).

AFTER TAKING the journey into the underworld to meet with Persephone, she is empowered, not the external power where we can dominate others, but a power that comes from within her very being.

The transformation process takes her from the innocence of a princess to the empowerment of a goddess. The creative processes of life can be fragile and mysterious, and there are times when Psyche knows she needs to wait until her creative gift is ready to be seen by others.

Psyche has learned to
~ Fly with her own wings and be guided by her own instinctual knowing.
~ Take heed of nature and be willing to live in tune with its cycles and flow in tune with her own rhythm of living.
~ Hear the small voices within and around her that have become her wise intuitive guides
~ Know she can gain help from a higher source.
~ Live from her centre, her inner flame of true focus.

By the end of her story, Psyche is grounded in her own being and aware of her intuitive and psychic wisdom, and she is beginning to recognise her healing powers too.

The power that comes from within her allows her to know and to speak her truth. The lessons that Psyche learns pave the way for her to become a confident, self-reliant, and self-reflective young woman.

Psyche, Eros, and the new life called Joy can be taken as elements of a single person's love of self as a soul. Psyche's journey is our transformational path also, connecting us to the creative flow as we become one with the river of life.

Psyche's lessons are lessons for us all. The qualities of the heroine are to have courage, to trust in guidance and to honour one's own inner wisdom.

- **Timing and Strategy**: Developing patience, timing, and the ability to be able to strategise.
- **Being Open**: Becoming conscious of guidance from a source greater than the self. Remember, it is universal intelligence and the mystery within all things that is both invisible and magical.
- **Learning to Listen**: Witnessing our strengthening powers of intuition and psychic knowing is how we strengthen our own sense of authority.
- **Trust**: Develop trust in our inner wisdom and our intuition and in an invisible higher intelligence.
- **Presence**: The quality of being fully present.
- **Boundaries**: Staying focused and saying no to the demands of others as we commit to our path; having the ability to set boundaries with others.
- **Commitment**: Holding true to our beliefs even when they may seem unattainable.
- **Simplicity**: Honouring truth and beauty so that life becomes simplified.
- **Natural Cycles**: Learning that change takes time, and there is importance in allowing a cycle to unfold in its own time.
- **Creativity**: Not forcing the birthing process, knowing that our creations reveal themselves when *they* are ready.
- **Darkness**: Developing a new relationship to mystery, knowing that darkness is our friend and invisibility is a gift. Being able to withdraw from the light of the midday sun into a connection with the wealth of wisdom contained within us becomes a treasure in our lives.
- **Transformation**: By facing the fear of death,

the ultimate letting go, we learn to trust in ourselves.
- **Connection**: Connecting to the ever-changing world and the ever flowing river of life. We know that it is Gaia, mother earth, that supports us, and the galaxy of stars and planets connects us to the mysteries of other worlds.
- **Value our Inner Wisdom**. We do not always know where our path will lead and yet we can have the trust to keep going, one step at a time. We uncover our true and authentic self as we learn to trust in our feelings and the subtle ways of sensing and perceiving with our instincts and intuitions.

THE HEROINE'S quest is motivated by a desire for love that takes her into the depths of the underworld where she becomes connected to her inner wisdom and receives guidance from nature and the universe.

Ultimately, the heroine's quest is a personal pathway into a deep connection with her soul.

Through our heroine's journey, we embodying our feminine powers and we find our true voice so we can express the truth of who we are. Magic happens when we live in the flow with our authentic soul-self. This is the path of individuation, which flows into maturity and connection with our inner truth. The outcome of this path is self-realisation.

We develop the ability to see that the simplest things in nature are able to assist and guide us. Living in rhythm with the flow of life and feeling a connection to nature, to the sacredness of the earth and all living things.

We know not to force the process of growth and when we become willing to surrender and risk life itself by letting go of old forms and perceptions of who we are, and being willing to be guided by that which can only be sensed on an emotional level and felt in our subtle body.

With this new sense of our feminine soul, feelings bubbles up from within, as we enter a place of innocence and newness. The light in our eyes shines as we live creatively in each ever-changing moment and our ultimate creation is the rebirth of joy.

After all, the words "psychic" and "psychology" are derivatives of "psyche" which means soul.

There are different ways in which we can receive psychic information from the realms of the great unconscious where cosmic soul resides. The four major ways of knowing are:

    clairaudience - clear hearing
    clairvoyance - clear seeing
    clairsentience - clear feeling or sensing
    claircognizance - clear knowing.

These ways of perceiving bring us as subtle messages that allow us to read beneath the surface and sense connections between all living things.

It is time to look with greater respect at our inner world of feelings, hunches, and body sensations. Attending to this inner world is the pathway to connect to our soul.

Upon my return home to New Zealand, I felt an inner calling to explore the essence of feminine energy. My reflections on the myth of Psyche heightened my awareness as I began to walk a new path; a process of listening to the messages from my heart and honouring the feminine ways of being. Through this process, inexplicable moments of insight, intuition, telepathy, and synchronicity unfold.

Sometimes though, I have felt as if my soul is lost and in those moments, I remember that the soul can easily be found, for it can never truly be lost at all.

The world supports me in magical ways when I allow my soul the freedom to fly into the beyond and to return again to me.

PART III

INTO THE DARKNESS: HIDDEN GIFTS
AND THE DARKLY VEILED FEMININE

La Vierge Noire

She is small, she is black, and she is hidden away
Her eyes seem still yet she gazes directly at me
She can see into the very centre of my being
Reading my truth, the essence of my soul

She psychically embraces me with her love
Blessing me with healing, making me whole
She knows all of me and I no longer feel
That I am invisible or have lost my way

Her presence is magnetic, deep and mysterious
She is alchemy: nature transforming itself
She is Dark Matter ~ Mother of us All

10

LA VIERGE NOIRE

THE BLACK VIRGIN AND CHILD

I HAVE MADE many trips back to France since my journey in 1989, each time starting and ending my journey in Villefranche-sur-Mer, the place where I saw my first Black Virgin statue at St-Jean-Cap-Ferrat.

I have often explored Provence, sometimes with friends, but only when I travel alone do I find myself in search of the ancient Black Virgin and Child statues that I have found hidden away in the crypts of churches.

In France, they call her *La Vierge Noire*, the Black Virgin. These Virgin and Child statues have grown into a secret fascination for me. But since I did not have the words to describe their meaning, nor did I understand their symbology, I kept my experiences to myself for many years.

The first statue I ever saw of La Vierge Noire was beside the Chapelle Saint-Hospice at Saint-Jean-Cap-Ferrat. Made of bronze, she stands beside the steeple, and at eleven meters high she towers above the rooftop of the church. She is a modern statue and was placed there in 1937 as an expression of thanks in honour of the healing blessings a family received from her.

This discovery began my quest, to search for the ancient Black Virgin statues that are hidden away all over France. Most of those I found are small statues of a woman holding a child, usually simple in design and black in colour although not always so. In ancient days, she was often carved from pear wood that has blackened over time.

There are terrible stories of happening to those who have tried to steal the statues or destroy them. There are stories, too, of how she has often been found in the branches of bushes by peasants long ago. It is interesting to me how she still resides in so many of the churches across Europe, and especially in France. If you go looking for her, you will find her ensconced in dark places with candles lit in her honour. It is as if she cannot be denied and yet cannot be fully acknowledged, either.

On a trip to the Camargue, just south of Arles, I visited L'Église des Saintes at Saintes-Maries-de-la-Mer (a town whose name translates ~ Saint Mary of the Sea).

There, deep in the crypt of the church, I found Saint Sarah the Black (Sara-la-Kali) holding her child. Mother and Child were finely dressed and surrounded by candles, and close by were crutches left behind by those who had been healed in her presence.

Once a year, this Black Virgin is brought up from the crypt and paraded through the streets; dressed in fine robes and wearing a crown, she and her child are taken down to the sea as part of the procession. This happens every year on the 24 of May, the feast day of the Romani gypsies in celebration of their patron saint. This was my first discovery of a *small Black Virgin statue*, and I am now on the hunt for them everywhere I go. Over the years, I would find many more each time I traveled in France.

ON A TRIP TO MARSEILLE, I walked up a steep path to the left of the horseshoe bay to a church called the Notre Dame de Confession. The church is perched on the hill overlooking the entrance to the magnificent harbour below. There, I found an ancient Black Virgin and Child sitting on a plinth on the wall in the crypt of the church. She was small, only ninety-eight centimetres high. She too is taken through the streets in procession on one special day of the year. On that day, she and her child are dressed in finery and given golden crowns, and many people gather together to be part of the celebrations.

IN CHURCHES in Arles and Aix-en-Provence, I have found unusual black statues—one where the child stands on a golden ball beside the Virgin, and another where the Virgin has a distorted, elongated right hand. I do not always understand the symbolism in these depictions.

AFTER A DAY SEARCHING IN AVIGNON, I was surprised to find a Black Virgin statue in the Notre Dame des Doms, the church beside the Palais des Papes in the centre of Avignon. She was locked away in the treasure room and could only be seen for one hour on certain days of the week, so I returned the next day at the appropriate hour. With the help of the guide, I finally located her on a high shelf under a glass dome. She was small and very old, and I felt so happy to have found her there in a city dominated by the patriarchal history of the Pope.

In a church in Limoux, the Basilique Notre-Dame de Marceille, I found the Vierge Noire at the left side of the altar. While I was there, I watched a man seated at a small table writing his thanks to her in the book that was provided for this purpose. He sat there for a long time, recording his story of appreciation for her blessings upon his life. When I spoke to him afterwards, he told me he was writing to thank Mary, mother of Jesus, for her healing blessings.

I BEGAN to question the true identity of this small black statue, for she seemed to be something other than the Virgin Mary to me. As I studied the photos of these Vierge Noire, I began to ask myself questions about the essential nature of the feminine that these statues represented. I recalled my feelings when I was in their presence, and began to wonder if her dark and hidden presence held a connection to the story of Mary Magdalene, the other woman in the life of Jesus. Could these Black Virgins be a sacred symbol of an ancient feminine presence still alive in France today?

THEMES around her presence emerged over time, that spoke to me of the place that the divine feminine has held in the social structure of our world. She is present in so many churches, and yet she is somewhat hidden or obscured. Sometimes, I searched only to find that the statue had been lost or stolen.

I DEVELOPED a fascination with the Black Virgin, and black as a healing energy. For centuries, that which is dark and feminine in nature has been misunderstood and mistrusted, and placed into a derogatory category by societal beliefs.

The feminine principle is a power and a mystery that is unable to be controlled or fully known and this has led to her becoming disempowered and demonised for many centuries. This mistrust in the feminine has lead to her power being feared by many.

When the Black Madonna looks at us, she sees into the heart of matter at the core of our being and perceives our truth. She knows this truth even if we hide it from ourselves. A truth that contains our unique gifts that give our life purpose and meaning.

WHILE STUDYING JUNGIAN PSYCHOLOGY, I was introduced to the books of Marion Woodman who writes about conscious femininity. Reading her book *The Pregnant Virgin* became a turning point for me in understanding my feminine self. She describes the potential energy of ~

> *"the Black Madonna...as the birth of creativity and the rebirth into a life of soul."*

> *"The Black Madonna,"* Woodman continues, *"is the patron saint of abandoned daughters who rejoice in their outcast state and can use it to renew the world."*

In this way, Woodman describes the paradox of rejection and rebirth, which gives us the freedom to live creatively from our own heart and gives our soul a chance to grow.

If the Black Virgin is the natural home for the rejected child, the outcast, and the gypsy, then she is the protector of Mary Magdalene and all those who have been unacknowledged, disowned, or unloved. I am sensing that the powers hidden in the Black Virgin are the qualities found in many faces of dark feminine, including Demeter, Persephone, Psyche, Isis, Lilith and Mary Magdalene.

THE ORIGINAL CREATION myth of Lilith and Adam has resurfaced in recent years, bringing her story into focus. Lilith was the original partner to Adam. She refused to be less than Adam choosing to leave him and to live alone rather than succumb to his need for superiority over her. Her need to be an equal to Adam led her to take up the life of an outsider, and she is said to have become a cave dweller who lived from a place of her inner truth. She knew that f she could not be an equal partner then she would rather be by herself.

But for leaving Adam, she has become demonised with the spread of fearfully distorted stories, and such stories have created generalised fears of her feminine powers.

Her story has drawn projections of fear from those who wish to denigrate her, to keep her powerless and under their control. In this way, misinformation of Lilith speaks of the cultural devaluation and disempowerment of the feminine, which has overshadowed our culture for many centuries.

MARY MAGDALENE HAS SIMILARLY BEEN a long-misunderstood outcast. For centuries, she was written about as a whore and denigrated by the church. During this time, all that was feminine was associated with negativity. Witch hunts became common in Europe and resulted in huge numbers of wise women being violently tortured and burned at the stake.

Many of them were the natural healers and wise women of the day. Memories of these horrific times have impacted us all, resulting in unconsciously held, generalised fear and mistrust of the feminine in a strongly patriarchal world.

Given this history, it is interesting how the Catholic Church has recently made a turn around and now reveres Mary Magdalene as a saint and honours her with her own feast day held on the 22 of July each year.

DURING THE THIRTEENTH CENTURY, similar persecutions were directed towards the Cathar people. The inquisitions of the Catholic Church became a scourge throughout Europe, condemning the Cathar as heretics.

There is much history in the Languedoc to show that the history of the Cathar is intertwined with the presence of Mary Magdalene and both were persecuted and forced to become hidden or invisible, beneath the earth to survive.

Some people refer to the Black Virgin as Mary, mother of Jesus, but I do not see her as Mary of the Immaculate Conception. Rather, she represents the feminine principle of Mary Magdalene and the humanness of the mother and child bond that symbolises the creative essence of the sacred feminine here on earth. She is made of ordinary pear wood and simply carved, and yet her meaning is far from simple for she represents the powerful, creative forces of the feminine.

Although she is often hidden away, I know that she is not forgotten and she cannot be destroyed. She lights our way through any darkness, and as a mother she represents the primary creative force in our world. She honours all creative processes and she knows darkness as her strength.
The Black Virgin is not afraid of this darkness; she

embraces it, and although she is often unseen and invisible to the world, often hidden, or veiled, she is also very present in this land of mystery that is France.

I have witnessed the way she is revered in France. There are stories of her being stolen and then reappearing again, and there are times when she and her Child are dressed in fine clothes, crowned, and paraded through the streets. She is honoured, protected, and worshipped; she is thought of as a protector and healer to us all. We can relate to her as a tangible expression of the dark feminine and her power.

OVER THE YEARS, I have grown to know she carries power contained within blackness and she symbolises love and intelligence that emanates from soul. Her qualities are essentially that of creativity, healing, and feminine wisdom; and invisibility is an essential part of her presence.

SHE ALSO POSSESSES GRACE, beauty and psychic knowing. Above all, she is at home in the realms of mystery and magic and all that is unseen and unknowable, for she is a personification of the primal essence of the sacred feminine.

OVER TIME, as the heroine sits with 'what is' without the need to change anything, she learns to trust the messages that come to her from deep within. The more she gives time to this experience of being witness to her inner world, the stronger these connections grow.

Giving ourselves the space and time to perceive through the feminine perspective is how we strengthen and honour her presence within us. The feminine understands what is real in a heartfelt sense. We need to protect, cherish, and give space and time to know her in our busy lives.

> We nurture our souls when we journey inwards
> and connect with the humanness of ourselves ~
> our instincts (inner drives), our intuition (inner
> knowing), the physicality of our body (form), our
> passion (inner fire), our emotions (feelings that flow)
> and our gut instincts (innate body wisdom).
> This allows us to gain resonance with
> the truth that lives in our hearts.

Going alone into the darkness of our inner being and connecting to the power and wisdom that is contained within our soul is the path of the heroine's journey and the path of maturation. It offers the freedom to be your unique self and create a life that is beautiful and magical in its authenticity.

CARL JUNG DESCRIBES THE SHADOW, saying it *represents that which we often hide from ourselves; and can contain the very best of ourselves.* Opening to our own darkness can be a healing experience and when another acknowledges the truth of who we are, we begin to claim this for ourselves.

The only person we can truly be is our unique and authentic self; this carries the essence of our power and our purpose. To claim this is the Black Virgin's message to us all.

These statues of the Black Virgin seated with a child on her lap, both wearing crowns, speak to the essence of the sacred feminine. They are a pair and I believe they symbolise the feminine forces of creativity that have the power to manifest from the invisible dimension of source.

THE BLACK VIRGIN appears to be both earthy and dark, with an all-seeing and all-knowing presence. Although she may often be hidden or veiled, she is also very present in this land. It is in France that I began to experience the power and mystery of the sacred feminine emanating all around.

> *The archetype of the dark sacred feminine*
> *represents an awakening presence that is*
> *the healing and empowered feminine.*
> *The Black Virgin personifies these qualities*
> *as she affirms that which is real and true*

This philosophy is emerging more fully into today's world, activating the powers of transformation within us.

> *The words "small," "black," and "feminine" are not evil.*
> *Rather, they are powerful beyond belief.*

QUALITIES OF THE DARK FEMININE

I AM BEGINNING to understand why my fascination with the dark aspects of the feminine expressed in the Black Virgins intrigue me so. Being so often hidden, I find myself reflecting on the statues' deeper meaning. I realise that for many years I have hidden my fascination with the Black Virgin statues, since for me they represent unacknowledged feminine power that is veiled in mystery.

I HAVE JOURNEYED along my path alone in search of my inner strength as a woman; a search that began a long time ago when I received a message while sitting on the banks of the river Aude in the tiny village of Alet-les-Bains.

This is a journey my soul has called me to take, and in the process of following these urgings, I have discovered so much about how to live guided by my feminine wisdom.

∼

LA VIERGE NOIRE STATUES, though small, simple, black, and often primitive in construction, represent the sacred feminine manifest into form. They are an archetypal symbol, thought by some to be as ancient as the mother goddess Isis of Egypt who existed since the beginning, when goddess cultures and mother-child relationships were honoured in the world. La Vierge Noire also relates back to the Christian myth of creation when Lilith was the first partner to Adam.

La Vierge Noire has spoken to me with her dark presence and her magnetic power.

*With the steady gaze of her eyes, she sees
through into the heart of matter.
She cuts to the truth that lies in our hearts
and resonates with our authenticity.*

*She understands the cycles of creation and
destruction, and the importance of the
incubation phase of creativity and birth.*

*She sees you, hears you, she knows the truth
of who you are. She can see into your heart,
feel your pain, and heal your wounds.
She validates your experiences and
loves you unconditionally.*

*She is virgin, whole unto herself.
She knows that it was never intended for her
to be less than her masculine counterpart,
but to compliment him as his equal.*

MANY PEOPLE associate darkness with negativity and fear. I now experience blackness as a place of potentiality, and the source from which creativity is born. There are different qualities of blackness: some are expressions of negative energy or illness in the body, but there is another blackness that can be used as a force for healing.

Barbara Brennan in her book *Hands of Light*, describes how she uncovered a quality of blackness as a healing force.

She describes how she uses black light, which she refers to as

> *"a velvet black, like black velvet silk. It is the black mystery of the unknown feminine within all of us, which teems with undifferentiated life."*

Brennan says this energy presence brings a feeling of oneness with the divine. To me, it is the very essence of the Creatrix that she is describing here:

> *"Sitting within the black velvet void is another way to be one with the creator, but this time without form. To sit within the black velvet void means sitting in silence and peace. It means completely being there, in fullness and without judgment.*
> *It means going into a state of grace."*

> *"A place of blackness where everything exists in potentiality— both past and future, and the now."*

Every woman who has been through an experience of giving birth knows that there are forces, which take over the physicality of her body and instinctually flow with rhythms of powerful movement. These forces are strong and unstoppable, and through them she is changed. It is this process of birthing a soul into physical existence that is an experience of magic and great wonderment.

The creation of any work of art that speaks to others and connects us to our soul also mirrors this process of birthing. The darkness that is the womb is the place where all new life is nurtured and allowed to grow; it is a place of creativity that unfolds out of darkness.

That which is in the spaces of our shadow and darkness needs to grow into the light so that we can develop a new relationship with these aspects within ourselves. Through this process, we become whole.

ALL NEW CREATION is conceived in blackness. It is where the initial creative spark, unites with the seeds of potentiality, and begins the miracle of something new. This requires incubation time within this state of blackness to be able to form and grow until it has developed enough to be born.

I perceive this blackness to be a place of great creative power in potentiality - as important as the light of the sun is to our existence. This blackness has a totally different quality than the light energy of the sun. Just as feminine energy has a totally different quality than masculine energy.

Blackness is the compliment to light, for both depend on each other for their existence. Although too much light or too much darkness can have negative consequences, we need both to harmonise and balance our lives. There is both mystery and magic contained within blackness, which we cannot see or fully understand.

The Chinese display this harmony and synthesis beautifully in their yin-yang symbol, showing that there is a centre of inner light within darkness and there is a centre of inner darkness with the light. In this way, it also shows that opposites always contain something of each other within.

IF LIGHT CAN BE SPLIT into all the colours of the rainbow when it passes through a prism, and a rainbow is a naturally occurring fractionation of light into all the colours we can see, then could it be possible that black holes contain all the colours of an alternative universe which we do not have the ability to perceive or comprehend?

I think of black holes as dimensions of potentiality, and an undifferentiated source; home beyond the death and rebirth of all form. If this black beyond our time-space universe is a place of primordial darkness, into which our stars dissolve, then could this also be a place of divine potentiality from which our world is continuously reborn?

Just as the cycle of birth and death is so familiar to us here on earth, we can see this on the cosmic level of our universe as well. It is in the nature of cycles that there is birth, growth, death, and then decay into formlessness, as in the seasons of nature and in the cycles of our cosmos.

While we devalue the feminine as a construct present in our patriarchal society, we fail to acknowledge the immensity of the dark creativity found in her birthing process—a process from which every human being has emerged into form.

ON THE EMERALD Tablet is written *"as above, so below."* Similarly, it is true that everything is reflected in everything.

What if darkness is not just the absence of light?
What if it is the counter balance to the powerful energy of our solar world and that it has an equivalent richness and value all of its own?

Could it be that one of the greatest paradoxes of life is that the creativity of rebirth comes from the place of greatest darkness rather that the place of light?

While we fear this blackness, we fear also the profound source of our creativity and the power of our feminine essence. The black feminine is related to psychic wholeness in myth, and to the pre-Christian gods of the Egyptian era whose deities Isis and Osiris are shown as black.

IF COLOUR CARRIES its own vibration, and if black is made up of all the colours together, does it then carry the energetic vibration of all things as pre-conscious potentiality.

I cannot see with my eyes when in total darkness; I only need to tune in with greater sensitivity to my surroundings to find my way. Using all my senses, my instinctual and other subtle realms of perception to navigate my environment.

Similarly, just because something is invisible does not mean that it does not exist or that it cannot be perceived in a way that is beyond our five senses.

For me, black carries a powerful energy vibration, and I sense hidden layers of depths beneath its surface. I remember wearing a black sweat top and feeling protected from mountain lions when I was camping in the foothills of the Sierra Nevada. At the time, I felt it gave me a degree of invisibility and an energy field as psychic protection so that I could move about without attracting attention from others. Later, it gave me a feeling of anonymity I found useful when I was in large cities like London, New York, or Melbourne.

FROM THE TIME I encountered La Vierge Noire statues, and then black as a healing energy, darkness has carried a mystery and magic for me. On one of the guided inner journeys I experienced when studying psychosynthesis, I connected to my spirit animal, the black panther. I grew to love the quiet power of my black panther, and when I journey deep into a dark forest, I find that I feel comfortably at home with my surroundings.

THE POWER, presence, and mystery of black energy resides in the invisible face of the feminine as a dimension beyond death and rebirth, I liken to a black hole in space. This is the dimension of Source where the alchemy of becoming resides as the unknowable dimensions of potentiality.

> *Are we able to conceive of the enormous creative potentiality that exists within black holes in the space-time continuum?*

THE CREATRIX as the feminine face of Source, encompasses a dimension that imagination reaches into and creativity emerges from. Her essence is that of veiled mystery and magic. She is the mystery of dark energy: with it is endless aliveness, but also endless stillness that coexist together.

I have sensed the presence of the sacred feminine as a powerful magnetic energy. The closest I can get to describe the quality of this invisible force is that of being in the path of a total solar eclipse; where all becomes dark, still, and cold, and yet there is an eerie kind of subtle light present in which one can perceive the outline of forms as dark shadows; and at the same time feel a magnetic force all around which is the pure essence of the moon illuminating with her presence.

AS I BEGIN to make friends with darkness and become

comfortable with the mystery of the unknowable, I find myself uncovering new ways of seeing, knowing, and making meaning of my world.

As I learn to trust in my inner guidance, I understand more than I ever did before. Intuitive wisdom helps me to weigh up my choices and make wise decisions. It reveals the way to go as my path unfolds before me, one small step at a time. Perceptions become heightened as my intuition strengthens. Like the lamp of the Hermit in the tarot, a light illuminates only the path I need to see before me of my road ahead.

BEING willing to travel into dark places can bring balance between the light and dark in our lives. It is time for a new relationship to this hidden realm; a time to value the feminine ways of knowing and to allow darkness to become our friend. In this process, that which has been denied, denigrated, and distorted can be reclaimed and transformed and the powerful energies of the Black Virgin can be restored.

Her essence is the energy of love that recognises the truth and beauty within every person. This feminine level of consciousness renews our awareness of the mysteries of the creativity of life itself and brings balance to our world.

There is a black that is negative, a black that is wise, and a velvet black that holds the power to heal and transform us

12

THE MOON'S LIGHT AND HER DARKNESS

My healing experience in Quillan made me aware of the moon's magnetic power when her light is at its fullest. Since then, the moon has become a clear expression of the natural flow of the feminine for me, and I now honour her phases as part of my everyday life.

Her cycle goes from a slither of a bright new moon in early evening and grows to her greatest shining light at the time of the full moon, then wanes until she becomes invisible in her dark moon phase. Her energy is always present, whether she is in her darkness or shining brightly and how we perceive her depends our place on the earth. We say that her light is the reflected light of the sun, but I know she has an energy that is all her own which can be felt and is other than the energy of the sun's reflected light.

∾

One afternoon while attending an Astrology Conference at Plymouth, Cornwall in August 1999, I experienced being in the path of a total solar eclipse. This day I experienced a tangibly different kind of darkness, with a magnetic quality to it. As my surroundings became eerily cold and quiet, the light of the sun began to disappear from the sky. The birds stopped singing and lined up along the peaks of the rooftops, sitting very still and the temperature dropped dramatically. I could see the world around me although it was a dark shadowland of magnetic blackness that came from the moon's subtle glow in her purest form.

At the time of a total solar eclipse, the magnetic energy of the moon becomes equal to the solar energy of the sun, creating a dark-lightness that represents a time of pre-birth that contains within it the seeds of new creation. There is a feeling of magic in the air in this powerful meeting place.

The first break of sunlight out of this darkness creates a point of light, a diamond sparkle then a ring of light reveals itself around the moon, and everything begins to shift as the warmth of daylight gently returns. This moment of magic is symbolic of the sacred marriage between the sun and the moon ~ referred to as the diamond.

IN ANCIENT TIMES, women used to gather together at the time of their menses, taking themselves away from their everyday lives and going into retreat. It was their time of shedding the old and preparing the ground to incubate the new.

This ritual showed that they were attuned to the cycles of death and rebirth in their bodies, and in the world of nature that surrounded them. They knew the magic of creation, for not a single human being exists without this magic that happens within a woman's body. It is for this reason we know the core essence of feminine is creativity.

When we repress this need in ourselves and do not allow time away from the bright lights to rest, recuperate, and reflect on all that is, we are denying the needs of our soul.

This inner time is so important: it allows time for us to connect to the heart of all matter and feed our soul.

ALTHOUGH THERE ARE times when actions in the outer world are important, we are not machines, we are souls and it is the relationship we have with ourselves that sets the tone of our lives. This relationship ultimately requires us to let go and trust in something greater than ourselves and be guided by our connection to universal wisdom and the intuitive and psychic knowing that lives within us.

WHEN WE SLEEP DEEPLY, we fall into a connection with the unconscious realms. While in this place we can process our experiences, solve our problems, uncover new pathways, and heal ourselves. Our dreams are a way for us to process all that is happening in and around us; a way of restoring our soul and providing guidance in our waking lives.

PSYCHOTHERAPY IS a pathway for us to enter into the dark places in us, with the help of a guide. In the processes of psychotherapy, we are guided to shine a light into the hidden parts of the self, which may be feared and disowned. As we bring them into the light of consciousness to be experienced, we create a deeper relationship to our inner world.

The phase of the dark moon is similar to the twelfth house in astrology: the place where ancestral memory resides and the unacknowledged parts of the self are hidden away. It is a place where we can lose ourselves in connection with the unconscious realms, symbolised by the oceans of our world; and where our dreams can connect us to the universal wisdom of the cosmos. This dimension of our existence where altered states, dreams, angels, and devils reside; is a place that calls us to develop our trust in something much larger than ourselves. Where our personal boundaries dissolve and we let go of our ego and flow in the currents of cosmic energies for a time, releasing our fears of the unknowable realms.

AWARENESS of the light of the moon's magnetic energy helps us reframe our concept of the moon and of the feminine.

Our perception that she is not there when we cannot see her is a false belief. She is present all the time, and her dark moon phase of invisibility is the most fertile, creative phase; and a necessary part of her existence that is reflected everywhere, in nature, the earth, and the cosmos.

As darkness becomes our friend and we expand our levels of perception into the invisible realms and see the moon as the embodiment of the creative essence of the feminine. Revisioning blackness, as I have done, gives a new understanding of the healing potential within blackness.

IT IS time to become aware of the power within invisibility, the presence within blackness, and to include mystery and magic as an essential part of the sacred feminine rather than fearing all that appears to be unknowable or mysterious.

The moon weaves her way across our night sky, and as she ends her old cycle and prepares to begin again, she becomes hidden in darkness and mystery. Invisibility is part of her charm and her magic. Our constant focus on the light does not allow us to appreciate the richness of the dark or value the invisibility required in the incubation phase of life.

We are taught not to value this dark time of retreat and yet this time is an invitation to take time out of our busy lives, to be still and rest in this shadow phase. It is a fertile time rich with gifts of creativity, wisdom, and healing. Although this dark phase can bring up a fear of being alone and a fear of death, these are aspects that must be faced on a soul quest.

I BELIEVE IN MAGIC. A caterpillar is born into a world where it focuses on the search for fresh, green leaves to munch on. It is magic when the caterpillar stops eating and curls itself into a ball, shedding its outer skin and becoming a chrysalis. The old form breaks down into its essence in the protected darkness of the outer container. This is the conjunction in alchemy where the magic of transformation begins.

There may be sadness with this loss of the old forms with the need to let go of what has been. This is a time of surrender and a time of waiting that cannot be rushed. Transformation will happen in its own time, from within this medium of incubation: a place where the soul can rest and wait until a renewal begins to manifest. This place where magic begins, is where we connect with the golden essence that is the truth and beauty of soul itself. Freedom and authenticity is reborn as a butterfly begins to emerge from the chrysalis, dries its wings, and takes flight.

EVERY BABY that is born into this world comes with a new promise and a chance to begin again. Every new creation carries this inheritance: the promise of a world reborn. Our child self brings the gift of innocence and wonder and a belief that anything is possible.

TRANSFORMATION CAN BE a painful process where all seems lost, yet its gifts can be beyond imagining. It is a time of letting go and waiting in the darkness, just as the caterpillar, at some point stops feeding and changes into a cocoon and waits for the time for rebirth to arrive.

In the chrysalis, the old form of the caterpillar completely breaks down in an amorphous liquid, allowing the process of alchemy to take place hidden behind the darkness of the outer shell. When the process is complete, a totally new form emerges - as a butterfly, more beautiful than all that preceded it. Magic has taken place behind the scenes in the invisible realms, and for this reason children find the story of the caterpillar and the butterfly fascinating and magical.

THIS SYMBOL of the butterfly represents psyche or soul. It needs a place of darkness and time to relax into a place where it is invisible and unknowable, while contained within a supportive container. This alchemical process with its own timing, is nature continuously dissolving and creating anew.

COULD the caterpillar have an intuitive knowledge that it can one day become a beautiful butterfly? The creative processes of life can be fragile and mysterious in the early stages. The creative gifts of the feminine has its own timing, and is the creative expression of the heart.

THE PROCESSES of transformation requires that we learn to trust in blackness as a place of nurture, healing, and immense creativity. This blackness, I have come to realise is the invisible aspect of nature and the essence of feminine power, the energy of death and rebirth, and the constant transform of life into our soul's creations. After all, the inquiries of physics are finding immense potentiality within the 'no-thingness' of black holes in space.

IT IS the darkness of the night sky that allows each star to sparkle, and reveals the shining luminescence of the moon. Without the blackness of the night, we would not be able to see the myriad stars in our cosmos. The darker and clearer the night sky, the more we can see a blanket of stars in the trillions. Sometimes, we forget that these stars exist when we cannot see them. It is now time for us to create a new relationship with darkness, as the complement of light.

DARK AND LIGHT are primal opposites and they are necessary to create our physical reality. They are a duality, which creates a state of tension as between earth and sky; moon and sun; feminine and masculine. It is this duality that is the positive and negative charge, a condition necessary for the creating the driving force necessary for our continued existence. In the terms of this duality ~

The Sun is golden, solar, fire - directed action
The Moon is silver, magnetic, water - circular movement

When we are willing to learn and grow, we move in spirals of increasing awareness that open us to new possibilities and connection to feminine creative forces.

The dark moon phase is the time to nurture
new creativity within the womb of life

Cave Dweller

I have been a cave dweller for many moons,
Unaccustomed to the noon day brightness.
There is comfort and safety in my hidden haven
And I rarely leave this place I now call home.

I have grown into the subtle shadows and deep darkness
Where I commune with my Hestia crone.
I love the quiet and the stillness
Where the voices of my soul dance around me.

There is a beauty and a truth in the essence of their song
And I know my being-ness matters.
My silence is not silence.
It is full of the voices of my soul singing
Listen and you will know how rich this quiet world is.

TIME IN MY CAVE

AT TIMES, I have felt called to travel to France in search of mystery and to understand my memories and déjà vu recollections. But instead, I have found myself being led into an inner world of self reflection that has impacted upon my sense of myself as a feminine woman.

I have become a cave dweller and I have learned to sit in the darkness of my not knowing. My cave has become my place of containment where I have the time and space needed to listen, to reflect, to be, and to imagine.

In this place I can incubate new impulses and reseed the pathway of my life by awakening to the potentiality of all that lies within me. Time in my cave has led me to my inner source of wisdom and I know that this time spent alone has been a necessary part of my becoming whole.

WITH MUCH OF the world focused on outer achievements, it takes both courage and a belief in something beyond our everyday concerns to be able to gift oneself the space for inner journeying.

Feelings of being alone, lost, and sometimes invisible have been familiar to me, and I have needed to be willing to let myself unravel and become lost, and accept my not knowing what may come next. Then I am able let go of all that has been, to listen inwardly and make space for a new reality to reveal itself to me.

GOING into the darkness of the unseen and unknowable is a risk I had to take, for in this is place of imagination, I have learned to trust in my intuition and the wisdom of my body.

By becoming a cave dweller, I am learning to surrender to the outcome and to hold a space open for other dimensions of universal intelligence to arise. As I get to know my inner child, my butterfly wings ~ a symbol of my transformation ~ to begin to grow.

EXPERIENCING loss has led me on a long and sometimes lonely journey, but also led me to the greatest of gifts. One of these gifts has been the coming home to my soul that opened me to a larger world and the ability to tap into the infinite potentiality that lives within the formless darkness, out of which new patterns arise into physical form.

This dark space of rest and retreat, where my psyche may enter into the world of dreams; and images can arise from unconscious realms. I can choose to travel into the past and into the future, and be fully present in the now.

I have joked to others that I work while I am sleeping, and for me it is true. I often awake with whole sentences that I quickly write down in the moment. They arrive as flashes of new insights that have a ring of truth to them that often astound me.

There have been times when I withdrew from life and retreated into my cave as a way to strengthen my connection to my inner cosmos and the creative forces around me. My soul became hungry for time and space just to be.

I have now learned to dip into my cave for short periods of time as a way to balance my inner and outer worlds, and I now love being in that place of reflection and solitude.

I have come to realise that I needed to lose my connection to my old self in order to enable me to journey into my soul self. My soul knows the truth of me and she has been longing to communicate with me in ways that I am able to receive.

When life is all about actions and achievement and there is no time given to inner reflection. When we fear losing control, we are not living from a place of love. Then the masculine ways are dominating our lives as we ignore our soul's messages. We are out of balance when we do not listen to the voice of our hearts, and we have lost our connection to our feminine soul.

I have learned to trust my own body wisdom and know the healing powers of nature found in dark places of the earth. As I sit with an open heart and honour the mystery of my existence, I imagine an underground river and a wellspring of the purest waters, with the ability to cleanse, heal and restore my inner virgin self.

I have grown to love this place of my cave, where the visible, hidden, and the invisible worlds commune with each other. It has become a source of guidance and nurturing and I know that the gifts of real change are an "inside job."

This inner world has become my home of insight, intuition, and the imaginings of my soul.

I now realise that I have spent many years seeking to know the essence of empowered feminine presence, so that she may take her place as an equal alongside the masculine.

The more I stay true to my essential core, the greater is my connection to my personal soul. It is as though all that I need to know is contained within me. I need only to listen to the messages that resonate within my heart. In the silence of solitude, I connect to my soul-self and hear voices which guide me to know my truth in each moment.

I HAVE COME to know courage as the willingness to face the unknown. Derived from the word "coeur" in French and "cor" in Latin, the ancient meaning of courage is "heart."

WITH COURAGE we can make new choices, create new habits, and set in motion a creative, transformative evolutionary energy force.

A way to know myself is to withdraw into my cave
to spend time in contemplation and reflection,
honouring the subtle wisdom of my soul

14

SOUL LANGUAGES

I AM A SOUL ON A JOURNEY, wanting to connect to my deepest longings and express the very essence of my being in a way that mirrors the inner truth in my heart and brings beauty and meaning to my world.

ASTROLOGY INTRODUCED me to universal elements, that spoke to a deep place within me. I began with the four elements of fire, earth, air, and water as ways to describe the diversity of our physical existence, and learned to translate these into the different ways we can connect to our soul. In Astrology, fire and air are considered to be masculine elements, and earth and water to be feminine.

FIRE IS OUR ENERGY BODY. The warmth of connection that fire provides is the spark of life force that activates our actions. This movement from our energy body, fuelled by our passion initiates our drive for self expression. In this way, fire is at the centre of our aliveness. It is our chi, the solar flame within us.

AIR IS OUR MENTAL BODY. It is the world of words, ideas, thoughts, concepts, constructs, and ways of understanding and making meaning of our experience. Air gives us the ability for abstract understanding and is a conduit for the power of thoughts, that carry the force of our intentions. Thoughts are now believed to be as real as our physical form. There is a power in words and power in telepathy.

EARTH IS OUR PHYSICAL BODY. The physical world is made up of tangible forms, which are embodied energy with instinctual intelligence. Our bodies speak to us and have a sensate consciousness that makes up our physical reality and is the ground of our being.

WATER IS OUR EMOTIONAL BODY. The emotions are the subtle and flowing and connect us to the world of dreams and psychic knowing, and emotional connection with each other. The water element like the oceans can wash over us with fluid and ever-changing movements that are not easy to contain. They give us the ability for sensitivity and empathy as well as a psychic awareness of other dimensions. They carry the relational powers of heart connection.

THERE IS a fifth element that is expressed as the subtle etheric energy body. This fifth element, extends beyond the physical body. It is an energy field known as the etheric body or Aura, which vibrates on a frequency that is faster than our physical energy body that we can see and touch. It contains a blueprint of our personal soul and exists in the invisible dimensions that are also part of our human energy system.

Using Reiki as a form of energy healing, it is possible to feel the etheric body through my hands. This subtle energy field is our psychic body. The word "psychic" refers to other realms of existence, whose messages may register in our etheric body and show changes in us before they manifest into our physical body.

THESE FIVE ELEMENTS correspond to the five points of the pentacle (star). This vibration of five is reflected in the pentacle, which is also the symbol of the feminine.

THE PENTACLE IS ALSO REFERRED to as the Venus flower, as the pattern that the planet Venus makes when she completes an eight-year cycle. This pentacle pattern shows the dynamic relationship between Venus and the Earth. Venus is considered to be feminine and carries the energy of love and Earth the connection to the ground of our being. The five points of the pentacle symbolise the heart energy of love and also represent the personal level of our individual soul consciousness

WHEN I WALK along my favourite beach, I become aware of all five elements surrounding me. I breathe the fresh sea air; my feet sink into the sand and fill the gaps between my toes. The water laps over my feet with the inflow and outflow as the waves caressing the shore, and the sun glistens across the water warming me. My etheric body expands as my light body intensifies, and I become relaxed and renewed.

THE LANGUAGES of soul are the ways in which the soul speaks directly to you through your mind, body, emotions, imagination and psychic levels of your experience. Speaking directly to your soul, sparks an inner light that awakens your personal soul and your connection with cosmic soul. If we can learn to trust in this soul language and experience it through all of the five elements, this opens us up to many ways of knowing.

The ways we experience our feminine wisdom are intuition, body speak, visions, emotions, and subtle etheric body sensations. Each of these guide us into soul consciousness.

We are each a unique expression of soul and the elements of fire, earth, air, water, and our personal sense of soul connect us with each other on the level of heart. Our soul is the mystery and magic of who we truly are, and our uniqueness as the sacred part of us that links us soul to soul.

The soul is not something to be found, for it is never lost. Rather it is we who have lost our connection to our soul. When we open the door to our inner self, we connect into our soul that lives at the heart of our being.

MINE HAS BEEN A JOURNEY, both inner and outer to find that which I believed to be lost. I now know my soul was always there, I just needed to connect within and learn to trust the magical, creative, and healing powers of my feminine soul, and learn the subtle language of my soul.

As I became curious about the mysterious and hidden dimensions of my reality, I want to understand the workings of the unconscious realms. My interest in psychology began to grow as I have found psychological theories that included the soul and were able to expand my awareness of other dimensions of consciousness. Studying these theories has given me ways to enrich the sense of soul that I seek.

After two years of experiential study at the Institute of Psychosynthesis, my interest in Jungian psychology began to grown as I immersed myself in the writings of Carl Jung and Marion Woodman. This married well with the psychological astrology I was learning. I found myself on a personal quest to uncover a sense of coming home to my soul-self, and these psychologies of soul were expanding my understanding of myself, as well as my place in the wider whole of humanity and the cosmos.

To some degree, psychological theories are a reflection of the theorist's own personality, and their perspective reflects the way in which they have made meaning of their world. Here is my brief take on two important twentieth-century thinkers who have written on psychologies of soul.

Roberto Assagioli, an Italian psychiatrist, developed psychosynthesis in 1926. His approach to psychology is a spiritual one that aims to develop a healthy personality with a centre of identity in the world and an expanded sense of self, which possesses an awareness that is both individual and universal. He developed ways to explore and integrate higher states of consciousness, as well as the develop a strong sense of personal boundary as a way to gain a more spacious sense of personal identity within a greater whole. Assagioli called his goal "self-actualisation." He focused on the right use of will and developed processes to allow for an expanded awareness of seven fields of consciousness.

PSYCHOSYNTHESIS HAS SHOWN me how to open the door to a meaningful relationship with my inner experience of myself, and to glimpse into the realms of higher consciousness. Through techniques of inner dialogue and visualisations, I learned to expand my sense of self and develop relationships to the many sub-personalities within me.

I also learned a meditation technique about being willing to sit in silence and stillness and to feel into the aliveness within that stillness. It is a meditation, which aims to connect us to the rich potential as energy within us.

As I learned about Psychosynthesis, I gave my attention to mind, body, emotions, imagination and my centre as part of my small self, and then expanded my awareness to my higher self. During this process, I became conscious of my personal boundaries, learned how to hold a point of tension between opposites and to hold space around the paradoxes of life, and I began to risk expressing how I felt in any given moment.

At each gathering at the Institute of Psychosynthesis, we would begin by sitting in a circle and each person would check in to the group by saying how they were in that moment. When my turn came, I would say something and then sit in a state of energy confusion, feeling vulnerable and very exposed. Over time, this experience taught me to sit with my emotions as a valid experience of my reality.

Until recently, I did not easily express myself in words. I had not found my voice and my innate shyness caused me great pain. As a child, I was very shy and quiet, not wanting to make waves or to upset anyone in the world around me. I had been able to express myself through dance but not through words. While studying psycho-synthesis however, I began to value my own inner experience as valid and meaningful, and I found words to express my experiences.

CARL JUNG, another founder of psychologies of the soul, gave us new concepts that became the basis of a modern twentieth-century Jungian psychology and showed us the pathway to individuation. He developed a rich inner life and he found that dreams contain valuable guidance and connect us to other realms of consciousness.

In his book *Memories, Dreams, Reflections,* he writes,

> "*I dedicate myself to service of the psyche. I loved it and hated it, but it was my greatest wealth.*" Later, Jung describes his work as being the "*cure of souls.*"

Jung used words such as **intuition, synchronicity**, the small **self** and **Self,** the **shadow, archetypes, individuation**, the **anima** and **animus**, which defined his new psychology of soul.

Today, they provide us with a language to describe the inner world of our psyche and expand our connection to soul and the collective unconscious. Words like **personal unconscious** and the **collective unconscious** have become common language in today's world, describing dimensions of past memories, ancestors, universal intelligence and an inner world of past and future together within the Universal consciousness of the Cosmos.

Carl Jung gave me a psychological language to describe my psyche, the unconscious, and gave validity to my subtle realms of experience. I now value the world of my imagination and the new insights I gain through my dreams. I understand synchronicity as a sign that I am living attuned to my centre and with the world around me. Jung validated both intuition and synchronicity, and their meaning-charged messages of authenticity and true guidance.

While studying Jungian psychology, I began to be aware of my shadow and my projections of that shadow onto the world around me. Jung's theory provided a way of interpreting my inner world that made sense to me.

Gradually, his psychology encouraged me to value my heart experiences with appreciation, gratitude, care, and compassion as a strength that nurtures me, and expand my sensitivity to subtle states of consciousness. In this process, I developed a language that connected my heart and brain.

We each have our own unique way of expressing the gifts hidden within us. This begins with finding and following our unique path of individuation.

He called the archetypal feminine principle that lives in the unconscious of men the **anima**, and the corresponding archetypal masculine principle in the unconscious of women, the **animus**. This was a way of describing the feminine as an invisible presence existing within men - this feminine perspective has the power to connect men to their inner world of soul that is essentially feminine. Jung describes the feminine principle as playing a role equal to that of the masculine in the process of alchemy.

Carl Jung held great concern for the death of a symbolic life and the effects it has on our lives, writing ~ it was a symbolic life that allowed him to feel a sense of the sacred.

By its very nature, establishing a relationship to the sacred feminine involves feeling into the dark and hidden places that live within us all. Jung understood this when he treated psychological experience as real—personally and collectively. Central to his thought is his claim that the inner path to enlightenment makes the darkness (the shadow) conscious.

BOTH OF THESE early twentieth-century psychologists valued the feminine at a time in society when feminine instincts and emotions were generally not trusted or valued.

At this time, many women who were not insane were placed in mental hospitals for an illness called hysteria: a common diagnosis for emotional outbursts in response to the repression of feelings.

These psychologies have helped me to validate my inner experiences, encouraging me to go within for my answers and expanding my awareness of the unconscious realms.

Both Carl Jung and Roberto Assagioli had in-depth knowledge of astrology that informed the way they saw the world. Astrology provided them with an awareness of our connectedness to everything around us. Above all, both thinkers were on a quest for wholeness by developing a relationship to the inner world, myths and symbols, the sacred and subconscious realms and beyond.

ARCHETYPES, symbols and art are a universal ways of connecting. They resonate with all people no matter which language they speak. Archetypes are universal patterns of experience that repeat across all races and cultures and are personifications of human experience. They resonate within us through the mediums of art, dance, imagery, and music, so we can communicate without the need for words.

～

ASTROLOGY IS a universal language of energy that has given me an awareness of the power contained within symbols that have carried archetypal meanings for men and women for thousands of years, connecting us with numinous mysteries and the accusal intelligence of the cosmos. Perhaps most obviously, symbols express a fundamental synchronicity in our personal and collective world.

THROUGH ASTROLOGY, I have come to understand the natural cycles that are continually unfolding as well as my unique place as an individual in the world around me. It has also taught me to understand the transpersonal themes emerging in the world as a whole. When I colour these symbols with myths and archetypal stories, they resonate in me on an emotional and soul level in a language all their own.

The power of archetypes has given me an expanded perspective of the repeating stories across history. Stories of myths and gods and goddesses have given me new colour, variety and depth of meaning to illustrate my own life story.

Over time, I began to understand the multifaceted dimensions of an individual and his or her relationship to the universal energies in each moment. I have a natural affinity for the depths of meaning contained within symbols, and this has led me to know myself and also understand why I have felt like an outsider for much of my life.

With four personal planets in Aquarius, I was destined to feel different and would have to find my own unique path.

My moon in Cancer, elevated in my natal chart, explains my sensitivity to fields of emotions and my desire to honour the feminine within me.

A strong Neptune on my ascendant explained my interest in the subtle realms of existence and why I have often felt unseen and misunderstood, as if invisible. Astrology's gifts of insight have become part of the very fabric of my life.

NEITHER JUNG nor Assagioli were comfortable with instincts, and did not trust them. But I know that any person who has faced a life-and-death moment, and any woman who has birthed a baby has felt the power and intelligence of instinct. To be taken over by instincts is to be superseded by a power far greater than our thinking mind, which has an intelligence that is wisdom and power. In those moments, there is no choice but to trust in this powerful guidance.

I thank Jung for his understanding of intuition, the unconscious realms, and the shadow. And I thank Assagioli for his experiential toolbox and expanded view of the unconscious realms. I also thank him for his theory of the right use of will, which I understand also as the power of clear intention.

ALONG MY JOURNEY, I found I needed to learn new languages that spoke from the whole of me. They expressed through my heart, my physical body, my emotional body, and awakened my centre of inner focus.

These languages have opened me to memories, and the

truth contained within. awakening my awareness of the blueprint that is a symbolic map of my unique, authentic soul.

Symbols, myths, and archetypes resonate in my psyche and their voices have come alive within me. They are the language that speak to my soul and help me to integrate the many experiences encountered along my soul's journey.

Symbols give us the power to recognise archetypal patterns, and make meaning of that which is invisible and beyond words

PART IV

THE LANGUEDOC AGAIN

The River Speaks

This river I sit beside speaks to me of the dance of life
It has a relentless, surging power and flow
That moves constantly onwards, as do our lives.
As I watch its gushing movements, I find the sounds
comforting as though it were a beloved companion

Water ripples over stony pebbles and rushes through
the gap between two large boulders,
Waves break around the boulders that disturb its path
Making ripples of white and blue and green while it
powerfully surges onwards below the surface and
then changes into a serene and gentle flow.

At the riverbank, some of the water swirl around
rocks to the left, some move forward brushing the sides of
the rocks on the other bank, some catch against boulders
or bank to turn and rush in the opposite direction
before resting in a pool of water. Still and going nowhere.

Then at last, moving on to join the flow again in a circular,
mini-whirlpool motion, rejoining the waters which open into
a widening riverbed. Further down, the river slows
and meanders more gently making swirling patterns,
as it passes the many hidden boulders in its path

How like my life this river is. With its times of tension,
drama and passion; its blocks and miss-directions;
Its whirlpools, waves, and stagnant hollows and then
the gentle meanderings, hardly noticeable,
when the water slowly moves again.
This river is clear and true and tells a tale of the
movements that are the journey of life itself

15

A CALL TO RETURN

It is 2011, and I have decided to revisit the southwest of France. I have been called back there by one of those unforgettably vivid dreams that stay in the memory forever and will not fade away. It was a dream that awoke a need in me to revisit this magical land that had spoken to my soul long ago and was calling to me yet again:

I am standing on the highest ramparts of a castle
looking down at a throng of people milling
around in the courtyard below.
It is nightfall and some are carrying flaming torches
to light the twilight hour. There is lots of commotion
amongst them and some appear very frightened.
There is a feeling of urgency in the air.

I am part of a small group of people standing apart
from the others. I know that most of the people
I am looking down on will be dead by the next day.
The guide says to me,
"It is time to go, we cannot delay a moment longer.
We must begin our descent."

*We are a small party of two guides, a Parfait and
myself, standing at the steepest part of the sheer wall
of the castle, looking down to the rocky undergrowth
of the hillside far below. We are 1,200 meters above
sea level and the mountainside is very steep.*

*I am a woman and I carry with me a book;
the Parfait carries scrolls. I am a Cathar and I know
it is important that we make our escape as we carry
with us spiritual writings, which must not be lost.*

*The drop below is terrifying but I do not have a choice.
I stow my book carefully inside my garments as I prepare to leave. I
must trust the guide and make my escape away from here now, for the
sake of all that my people believe in.*

This dream broke through into my semi-consciousness with vivid colours and disturbing emotions and I knew that I was witnessing a time of crisis and imminent danger for all around me. The mood was heavy and the people were preparing for their final hours. I felt that I was part of a tragic time that happened many centuries ago.

This dream stirred up intense emotions and a sense of déjà vu as the imagery recalled a time when the Cathar reigned in the southwest of France. Somehow, I had a strong sense that I had lived in that same castle at this time of great unrest long ago.

A myriad questions arose in me, and I felt called to return to the Languedoc: the place where twenty-two years earlier, my life began to change in ways so subtle and yet so meaningful, opening me up to another world.

Until this time, I had no thoughts of ever going back to visit the place that became the turning point between my old self and my soul self. I am older now, and I have spent many years making meaning of my experiences of that earlier time when the boundaries blurred between what is an inner thought and an outer experience. And so I find myself travelling to the Languedoc some twenty-two years or eight centuries later.

I BOARD the train to the village of Quillan. It is a small train but more modern than I remember, and as I step into the carriage I am greeted by a bevy of older women who are all excited to be sharing an adventure together. There are at least ten of them in all shapes and sizes, and one with a hairstyle that defies description. The sounds of their happiness seem like a good omen to me of my journey ahead. As the train moves on, they become more settled and begin producing tins of goodies to share around the group that hums with convivial conversation. By the time we reach Limoux, I am enjoying their foodie treats too.

The rest of the journey passes quickly and we arrive at the last stop, the train station in Quillan. I have booked a house for a month—a full moon cycle—on the edge of the village, an easy walk from the station. Once settled, I find myself looking out towards the Pyrénées that border the lands of France and Spain, and pondering my need to discover if I can recall more clearly having lived here in a past life.

My plan is to visit the ancient Cathar castles to see whether standing on the highest parts of their ruins sparks a memory or a sense of déjà vu that brings my dream alive, or maybe even a recall of a richer memory of an ancient time.

I wonder, is it Montségur that is calling me from an ancient past? Could I have lived in this land many centuries ago?

Until now, my journey has been taken alone. It has been a search to find my inner strength and empowerment as a woman of soul, and it began with a message that came to me a long time ago while sitting on the banks of the river Aude in the tiny village of Alet-les-Bains, a village not far from this town. I am revisiting this magical land where the river spoke to my soul, but this time I am no longer journeying alone. I find myself accompanied by good friends. I have entered the third phase of my life and I now seem able to uncover the deep meanings of powerful synchronicities, which continue to guide my life. Synchronicities that have gracefully brought me to this place at this time.

A few days later, my Swedish friend Carina arrives and we settle into the three-storied apartment. The apartment is spacious, with a bedroom and bathroom on each of the upper floors, and living room with kitchen on the ground floor.

We open a bottle of Blanquette, a specialty of the area, to celebrate the beginning of our adventure together. The nearby town of Saint-Hilaire is where the monks discovered how to make wine with bubbles and long ago created Blanquette, a precursor to champagne.

We are enjoying a classic French breakfast of croissants and coffee in the courtyard, looking out over the valley beside the village of Quillan. We are both eager to begin our travels in the little hire car parked just outside our door. Carina seems happy to follow my lead and explore the countryside of this far western part of southern France.

"So, where to today?" Carina asks while we slurp the last dregs of our morning coffees.

"We'll go to Montségur today. It will take some time to get there, so let's get going as soon as we can. This is a place that may have called to me from an ancient past."

"Okay," says Carina. "You can tell me more about it while we are driving."

We are soon on the road heading south along the route to Mirepoix. It is Carina's task to remind me to drive on the right-hand side of the road, in case I have a lapse in concentration and forget. I begin to tell Carina my dream and then the story of the Cathar: how after being under siege for seven months in their castle high atop a mountain, they surrendered and gave up their stronghold.

MONTSÉGUR, the place we are heading to, is known as the site of the Cathars' last stand. The Catholics gave the Cathar a choice to convert or to die, so two hundred and ten Cathar made the choice to come dancing and singing down their mountainside and throw themselves onto the pyre of flames at the foot of the mountain.

After navigating a steep and winding road, we arrive at the castle of Montségur. We find ourselves climbing a ragged pathway to the top of the mountain to enter the ruins of the castle. Carina says that she feels like a mountain goat scaling a steep pathway, and I feel like one too. I understand now exactly why I am climbing to reach this treacherous and rocky mountainous stronghold: I see the image of a goat, the symbol for Capricorn, and realise that according to astro cartography, I am on my Jupiter line at nineteen degrees of Capricorn that falls across this longitude.

As I stand within the ancient walls of the Montségur castle, I see the sheer drop of 1,200 feet from the highest ramparts. If this is the place of my dream, I can see no way it would have been possible to exit by scaling the wall. I knew I was a female Parfait at that time, and I think now that there must have been a secret escape tunnel. Being here has not answered he mystery of how I made my escape.

I ask a tour guide about the age of the castle and learn that it was a ruin that has been rebuilt in recent times in honour of the Cathar who lived and died here. So maybe the wall was not as high, or there may have been secret tunnels that they used to get the supplies they would have needed to survive for seven months under siege. The view from the highest ramparts out across the distant lands is impressive, but it is the view into the enclosed courtyard just below that strikes a chord of meaning in my heart.

There, on the carpet of green grass, is a large heart-shaped curve of white stones with the form of a cross beside it. It is the energy of the heart and the equal-sided cross of matter that symbolises the philosophy of the Cathar. They believed that it was possible to lead a spiritual life without the need of a priest as intermediary, and that women as well as men could be spiritual leaders in their communities.

Every day that I am in France, I find myself beginning to sense the presence of the feminine more strongly. I am discovering that there are many Cathar strongholds in this region, and that some of the Cathar survived after the massacre at Montségur. I learn that the two castles called Puilaurens and Quéribus are where the Cathar surrendered some ten years after the fall of Montségur in 1244. Any of these castles could have been the place of the scene in my dream.

The next day, we visit Peyrepertuse castle, another stronghold near to the village of Cucugnan. Upon arriving, we discover that like the other castles, much has been rebuilt over the years. After our strenuous climb to stand within the walls of Peyrepertuse, again we look out across the land in all directions. These castles are impressive with their commanding views.

We travel to the nearby village of Cucugnan to stop for a late lunch, and find a table in a courtyard that is shaded by the dappled light of tall trees and after a refreshing salad, we set off to find L'Église de Cucugnan.

L'Église de Cucugnan is a very unusual church, unlike any other I have ever seen. It has a softness of golden light emanating all around, and I can feel the presence of feminine energy even before I enter the church.

The tree with branches of gold outside the church was the first clue that this place was different. Inside, the floors are terracotta, the walls are of the palest pink, and there are crystal chandeliers hanging from the ceiling. With a statue of a woman on one side of the altar and a man on the other, and a woman on the back wall above the altar taking centre stage, the church gives the flavour of glowing feminine energy. Each of the figures is dressed in golden garments, but it is the little statue of the golden woman just to the right of the main altar that catches my eye.

In an alcove protected with a glass screen stands *La Vierge Enceinte*, a woman dressed in gold and pregnant with child. Her left foot rests on the head of an angel, and below the angel is a crescent moon and a snake. She is a young woman carrying within her the rounded potentiality of her creative powers, and she is beautiful. She is made of gilded wood and she stands fifty centimetres high, glowing in her golden gown. To her right is a larger statue of a Virgin and Child, she also wears a golden gown and a crown.

La Vierge Enceinte is a well-travelled tiny statue, and is considered important because of its rarity. For a time, she was taken for display in an art museum in Carcassonne then later she was taken to Lourdes. From there, she was stolen and later found stored at the train station in Lille. Finally, she has been returned to Cucugnan where she is kept safely in a nook behind a see-through barrier. This small statue speaks to me of the joyful feminine energy of Mary Magdalene, for there are stories in this region of her presence here long ago, and rumours of her having had a child.

Rather than answering my questions of past life experiences, this dream that called me back is now leading me into new experiences of feminine presence here in the Languedoc. Even the room I sleep in has walls of the palest pink. For me, this return journey is becoming about a new connection to my feminine self: that part of me that has felt wounded, invisible, undervalued, unacknowledged, and unloved.

I am beginning to ask myself simple questions about the truth and beauty that lies within my heart as a way of uncovering the loving and creative presence of the feminine that I know has the power to feed my soul.

Eventually, Carina returns to Sweden and I find myself alone. The river is calling to me, and it is time for me to revisit Alet-les-Bains.

My dream calls me to revisit the Languedoc, Awakening me to experiences of an ancient past

16

ALET-LES-BAINS

AND THE ANGEL SANCTUARY

THERE IS something about rivers in France that stir the depths of my soul. I now return to Alet-les-Bains, and take some time to sit again and listen to the voices of the river Aude—the same river where I awakened to the voice of my soul many years before.

I become a witness to the river's constantly moving water, the boulders on the shoreline, the gentle breeze, the sun shining above, the swirling sounds of the water and all four elements come together and speak to me again. The river seems magical as it dances and sparkles and sunlight glitters upon its wavering surface and its song calls out to me as it races along.

I feel an excitement in the air that carries a promise of secrets yet to be uncovered. I begin to relax and my mind relaxes too, as I recall the dream that will not fade from my memory. This river stirs a knowing in me that I have lived here in another age. Maybe this is why I feel so at home in the south west of France.

I begin to notice that much has changed in this small village. The Hôtel l'Evêché has expanded and the gardens have matured, with tall trees giving shelter to the many tables and chairs scattered across the lawn. I find that I can no longer wander down to the river bank beside the ruins of the old cathedral, for they are walled off now and have become a tourist attraction open only for a few hours a day.

As I watch the river, I begin to think about my desire to meet with Henry Lincoln, the co-author of *The Holy Blood and the Holy Grail*. He is an expert on the sacred geometry of this land and has studied the mystery of Rennes-le-Château for years. I had emailed him to arrange a meeting but found that he was busy as a guide for a sacred tour.

As I walk back through the gardens of the hotel, I notice a bearded man seated at a table with a large map laid out before him with a group of intense listeners looking on. Suddenly, I have the thought that this could be Henry, and I approach the group.

"Are you Henry Lincoln, by any chance?" I ask in French. He replies to me that he is. I explain that I tried to contact him, and that I am on a return visit to Rennes-le-Château and that I stayed here twenty-two years earlier.

He exclaims,
"Twenty-two! Are you aware that this number is found throughout Rennes-le-Château and in the church of Mary Magdalene, and that it is the powerful number of the divine feminine?"

I would love to ask him more, but his group needs his attention and so I go on my way again, following along the river's path. How wonderful to have crossed paths with him if only for a few minutes. I leave with food for thought about the number 22 and the feminine presence I am sensing so strongly in this magical place.

∼

A SHORT STROLL further along the riverside, I discover La

Galerie des Anges, was not been there on my earlier visit so long ago. This is a spiritual meeting place called the Healing Angel Sanctuary, created by an Irish couple, Lorraine and Eugene, and housed in a building where the old thermal baths of Roman times had been.

There are many rooms in the building, each one showing Lorrie's angel artworks. A chair has been placed in front of each picture for visitors to sit and contemplate. The images are ethereal expressions of soul energy in many hues of colour and form that Lorraine has been guided to create. Each has its name and meaning written below. I am very taken by the "Glimpse of an Angel" and the "Breakthrough Angel" images.

> As I sit and meditate in front of
> the *Angel of Manifestation,*
> I reflect on the story of the Black Virgin.
> I can feel the sadness of her losses
> and the presence of her power.

Lorraine has been inspired to create these images, and she has set up this beautiful and restful sanctuary where her images speak to whoever takes the time to open to receive from them.

This angel sanctuary was a place of healing in Roman times, and in the centre of the building there is a fountain of pure spring waters that bubble up from the earth below.

I later discover that this area is actually the site of an underground lake, the second largest in France, an area where many healing springs can be found.

Further on in my stroll, I visit a church beside the ruins of a cathedral and find another small Black Virgin statue housed safely in an alcove behind a metal grid. So often, I am finding that the Black Virgin is present where there is an underground source of water, a spring or well that has pure and virginal water that can heal the body and the soul.

I am beginning to understand that the Cathar history is connected to all that Mary Magdalene represents, and this place is where the river Aude and the river Sals join each other at Couiza and Alet-les-Bains, close to the hills where Rennes-le-Château stands. There are many churches that carry the name of Mary Magdalene in the Aude region, and many Black Virgins with Child statues to be found.

The Magdalene Line, also called the Rose Line, falls through this part of France and on down into Spain. It is on this line that I feel the presence of the feminine strongly, as well as the healing waters that are an essential part of her presence. This is a place where it feels very natural to take time to just be with myself in an open and reflective way. It is here, too, that nature speaks to my heart and moves me with its beauty. I allow time for the flow of my emotions to surface as I think of myself in tune with the river of life: flowing and yet centred, aware of my physical presence, my intuitive knowing, and my psychic connection to source.

I sit and give myself space to connect into my feelings as they bubble to the surface of my consciousness and I gain clarity from honouring what arises from within me. My feelings are authentic, loving, and real. My inner relationship is reflected back to me by my experiences of the world around me.

As I become more trusting, I also become willing to act spontaneously, to follow the impulses that arise from a place of inner truth. As I listen to my inner voice and I gain insights that come from my intuition. I find that the deepest, darkest places hold the purest light of truth, and the greatest gifts. I nurture this place of inner light with attention, as a space that is pure and true for me. I have learned to live from this place of inspiration, connected to the energy of creativity and love that flows through me.

I hear stories of people called to move to southwest France, who have experienced magic, mystery, creativity, and healing. They experience mysterious messages, and some say they have sensed the presence of Mary Magdalene while in this part of France. It is possible, then, that the pure underground waters—wherever they are found—also represent places where the presence of the sacred feminine can also be felt.

Places of high energy, ley lines in the land, and springs where pure water arises from the depths of the earth are also places of sacred feminine presence

17

RENNES-LE-CHÂTEAU

AND MARY MAGDALENE

OVER THE NEXT FEW WEEKS, I make several visits to Rennes-le-Château, a village on a mountain with panoramic views in all directions. Rennes-le-Château has now become famous and many come to visit to find the source of the mysterious wealth that Bérenger Saunière found there. When I first visited in 1989, I was drawn to know about this mystery, and I found the energy of Mary Magdalene present in this place.

When I enter this church again, what strikes me most is that in low relief on the altar is an image of Mary Magdalene sitting with a book on her lap and a skull beside her. This suggests to me symbols of the death of Jesus and his teachings contained in the book of love that she holds.

To the left of the altar is a statue of Saint Joseph holding a child, and to the right is a statue of a Virgin and Child.

There are other statues of women, too—Saint Germaine, a shepherdess with her two sheep, and Saint Madeleine with a skull, book, goblet, and staff.

I notice that each of the male statues is accompanied with an animal or a child. Saint Anthony has a pig; Saint

Roche has a wound on his thigh and dogs beside him. Another Saint Antoine and Saint Joseph each with a child.

The stained-glass windows also have interesting stories to tell. Two of them show a man and two women with halos above their heads, and the second window shows a man and woman and also includes a hermit in a cave. The third window shows five men and a woman seated around a table. The presence of the feminine and the child is prominent here.

In the church garden, I find the grave of François Bérenger Saunière with these words carved into the head stone:

> Marie-Madeleine – L'énergie Divine Féminine
> François Bérenger Saunière
> 11 April 1852 – 22 January 1917

I am discovering that Mary Magdalene's presence is a major theme connecting me to the mystery and magic of Rennes-le-Château.

Mary Magdalene is said to have lived in caves at Sainte-Baume, France, but I feel her presence here too. I believe she was a divine expression of the sacred feminine, and that her energy is resurfacing again into world consciousness. Her energy is reviving the qualities of her presence as expressions of pure feminine essence that is both ancient and new.

In the Languedoc there are many churches dedicated to Mary Magdalene. Magdala means tower, and there are many towers here also that are rounded observatories, including the one at Rennes-le-Château which Bérenger Saunière used as a library and watch tower. Feminine symbolism and sacred geometry are present in this land, too. The five points of the pentacle is a symbol of Venus and this pattern can be seen as high points on the land, with La

Pique at the centre near to Rennes-le-Château. The powerful master number twenty-two is echoed all around Rennes-le-Château as well, symbolising the presence of the sacred feminine.

For this energy of the divine feminine to grow in our consciousness, we need to empower it with love and trust. Mary Magdalene, who lived her life believing in a true heart, spoke with her voice of love and carried the wisdom of the book of love within her. There are many who believe she was here and that her knowledge became intertwined the guiding principles of the Cathar in southern France.

CARINA LEFT FOR SWEDEN YESTERDAY, and this morning I find that I am missing her company. I no longer have the rental car and I have run out of coffee, so I decide to walk into the town square to enjoy a morning coffee. When I arrive, I find that I do not feel like having coffee in one of the cafés there, so I buy an apricot croissant from a small Patisserie and kept walking.

I soon chance upon a brocante shop selling an array of antique furniture and objets d'art. It is open and the owner introduces herself as Joanna and invites me in. As I enter, I smell the wonderful aroma of freshly brewed coffee. I ask Joanna if she sells coffee and she answers *"yes I do and it will be ready in a just few minutes."* With that, I find a chair in the inner courtyard garden.

There is another customer who over hears the suggestion of the coffee and asks if she can join me. Diane then sits at my table and we begin to talk. Soon after our meeting, I am rushing back to my apartment to collect a carry bag and camera, and to change my shoes.

Within a short time, we are in Diane's rental car heading towards Rennes-le-Château to explore more of the village.

Diane seems to know people at the village restaurant where we sit enjoying lunch discussing our shared interest in this mysterious place. There is a happy atmosphere and I feel blessed to have made a new friend.

A few days later, we tour farther afield with Diane's friend Rogier who takes us into the Ariège region, and somewhere near Foix we find a huge stone balanced on the edge of a high plateau with magnificent vistas of the Pyrenees mountains far in the distance. This stone is called the Sem Stone.

Diane lies on top of the Sem Stone, which makes her appear small like a blip on the horizon. I sit on the ground with the huge stone before me with the valleys and hills towards Spain as a backdrop. I rest quietly, allowing myself to just sit and listen, enjoying this magical place. The sun is shining onto my left side, and I can feel a warmth reaching right into my heart. It is a gentle nurturing feeling. And then I hear these words,

"I can love being a woman."

I feel these words are telling to me that it is okay to love being feminine and to give attention to my feelings. This message seems to be giving me permission to embrace the feminine parts of myself with love and enjoyment.

Later that day, we visit a grotto where a cathedral once stood proud on the land. In a bramble-covered field we discover not one but two grottos, which appear to be very old. Inside one is a statue of a man but the entrance is barred with barbed wire, and I decide not to enter. Inside the other, hidden away deep in darkness is a life-sized statue of a woman, sitting and looking pensively into a small heart-shaped rock pool. She appears to carry a sadness about her. I find out that she is called the Lady of the Mountain: here again, I find a feminine presence hidden away as if forgotten. This is becoming a major theme on my journey.

As I come out of the grotto, a beautiful bird with a flowing tail flies across my path and sits in a nearby tree. My companions do not see this bird. Then I find a very large pattern marked out in stone on the ground in the shape of bird's wings spread wide where the altar of the old cathedral had been. There is little else to suggest a cathedral ever stood here.

Earlier, I bought a postcard showing the outline of a bird called the Minerva, which is said to be a symbol of the Cathar. To me, the bird is a symbol of the freedom that comes from claiming one's truth: the gift to be visible rather than hidden, and to be seen for who you truly are, in a way that carries the ring of authenticity. And yet there is a price to pay for that as well. There is something to be said for not always being visible, for I am finding that to be fully in touch with the feminine energy requires both times of retreat and inner reflection as well as times of being visibly presence in the outer world.

When the feminine is present as the archetype of the queen rather than the princess, she carries a gracious strength and wisdom. Gentleness and caring are her nurturing qualities; intuitive knowing and inner guidance are her ways. Her way is the path of love, and this force guides her to follow the truth of her heart. This truth is the medium of magnetism that is expressed through emotions that is a force that joins hearts together in a way that is far more powerful than anything else in our universe.

Again, in France, I find my feminine self comes alive. I am learning to become open and receptive to her presence.

The next day, Diane and I visit Saint-Hilaire. As we enter the cloisters, we both see on the floor in front of us an image of a sword engraved in stone. Looking at each other, we say in unison, *"We can put down our swords."*

We both knew in that moment that we could call on the power of our swords should we need them and we could also chose to put them aside. We know to use the power of our swords with skill with discrimination - how to set boundaries and to choose our battles wisely. The sword represents the ability to cut through to the truth in all things, allowing us to use our minds effectively, to express our needs, and to cut away that which no longer serve us.

I have since discovered an image of a goddess holding the *Sword of Light*. She knows how to use her sword to cut through to the truth. She is a feminine archetype of this power that I liken to that of Excalibur, the sword in the King Arthur legends: *only the true in heart can release the sword from the stone*.

There is something about southern France that stirs my heart and resonates with the feminine within me. The possibility of past lives and familiarity to places and times gone by are unexplainable, and yet they surface for me here. I feel Mary Magdalene's energy is being reborn into many of our lives in today's world.

My soul is moved by the beauty around me. Images, words, the river's song and the rising moon are all expressions of the divinity and sacredness of feminine essence that connect me to my soul. I am finding my voice and I am learning that I can shine the magnetic light that is my feminine power.

Some believe that Mary Magdalene once lived in the Languedoc, and many have felt called to this land of mystery and presence of the sacred feminine

HONOURING THE BLACK VIRGIN

I HAVE MADE many trips to France and I find myself on the hunt for yet another ancient statue of the Black Virgin and Child when I am travelling alone. Often I find her locked away or she is missing, and sometimes I am unable to gain access to see her. Themes are emerging over the course of my travels that make me question the place the sacred feminine has held in our world.

IT IS NOW 2011, and on this return visit to France I begin to discover the Black Virgin in places of prominence throughout the country, where she is openly honoured in the upper churches ~ in Chartres Cathedral near Paris, and at the Notre-Dame de la Daurade in Toulouse. There is another famous Black Virgin in Montserrat Abbey near Barcelona. All three churches have been ancient sites of worship, and all three are found near to the Magdalene Line.

The Magdalene Line falls through Paris and down to Montségur, between Carcassonne and Toulouse, and then on to Montserrat in Spain. It is on this ley line that highly charged earth energies radiate their powerful forces that affect the subtle bodies of sensitive people. It is near this line that I experience an intuitive awareness of the dark feminine, awakening in me and I feel her presence in nature as it speaks to my heart and moves me with its beauty and truth.

I VISIT Avignon again and it is a joy for me to discover the Black Virgin's presence even in this very masculine city. The Pope's residence from 1309 to 1377, the Papal palace dominates the large square at the centre of the city.

A church informally called "the Dom" sits in the large square to the left of the Papal palace. It has a golden statue of a woman standing high upon the spire, and she is said to watch over Avignon and the place of Popes.

In the Dom there is a treasure room and there, high up on a shelf under a glass dome, I find a small and ancient black statue of a Virgin and Child.

Until recently, I had found her hidden away below ground, and now I find her locked away in this room of treasures.

But it was my visit to Chartres that really made me realise how often the Black Virgin is locked away and hidden below ground. I found three Vierge Noire at Chartres Cathedral.

The first is displayed in the main cathedral on a high pillar, surrounded by saints, with her own set of pews where people can take time to pray to her. Here she is openly worshipped by many. I noticed an old lady kissing the pillar that supported the statue, and then join the many others in prayer alongside the rows of candles lit in her honour.

There is also a statue of the Virgin and Child on the façade over the west front entrance to the cathedral. This western entrance is symbolic of the gate of birth and the sculpture of Mother and Child is called the *Virgini Pariturae*, meaning "virgin about to give birth."

The other more ancient Vierge Noire is locked away *sous la terre* in the crypt of the cathedral. I wait with my ticket in hand, bought from the bookshop at the other side of the grand square, until the appointed hour that afternoon when there is to be a guided tour through the crypt. This Black Virgin and Child, resides in the lower church of the cathedral, securely locked away and we are allowed to visit this mysterious crypt for a short time only.

That afternoon, I joined a small group and was shown on a guided tour through the underground passageways of the crypt. What I discover is the black virgin and her child sitting centre stage on her throne, they both are crowned and there is an altar before her and rows of seats facing her altar. There is a colourful tapestry behind her and a stained-glass window to her left. It is a place of worship where she and her child sit enthroned in pride of place within their own small chapel.

I am told that it is possible that her history dates back to ancient times that are pre-Christian. This site is thought to have once been a Pagan Sanctuary consecrated to the Mother Goddess and a Druid place of worship before the cathedral was built. There is also a well in this crypt. Again, I find that the Black Virgin near a source of pure water, confirming that water is part of her essential nature.

We are being rushed through this visit to the crypt and so I pause briefly to take more photos of the altar and the Black Virgin and Child in the dim light. I hear the clang of the gates closing, so I rush for the entrance, fearing being locked in for the night and I am the last visitor to leave as the gates slam shut behind me.

This lower church is different to any of the crypts I had visited before. There are stories of this lower church being a place where ceremonies of initiation had been held and telluric powers could be felt.

This Black Virgin and Child found is called "Notre-Dame de sous-terre, Our Lady of Underground," and she depicts the ancient great mother goddess known by many names including that of Isis of Egypt. She sits enthroned in her underground chapel. I had only a glimpse of this powerful archetypal feminine before she was quickly locked away. Similarly, I was not able to walk the labyrinth path on the floor of the upper church as it was masked by rows of chairs.

THE BLACK VIRGIN and Child represents many things to many people, and I now know her ways for she has spoken to me.

I believe she represents an ancient primal force that is the power of the feminine and she can awaken these hidden qualities within us through the quality of her presence.

I am learning to embody the energies of the Black Virgin and unveil her as an archetypal symbol of the sacred feminine. She is a force that can no longer be denied.

IN HIS BOOK *The Cult of the Black Virgin*, Ean Begg writes,

> *"our ancient, battered, much-loved, little-understood Black Virgins are a still-living archetypal image that lies at the heart of our civilisation and has a message for us. The feminine principle is not a theory but real and it has a will of its own which we ignore at our peril.......*
>
> *As the spirit of light in darkness, she comes to break the chains of those who live in the prison of unconsciousness and restore*

them to their true home. In the trackless forest she is both the underground magnetism and the intuition that senses it, pointing the traveller in the right direction."

That she is called the Virgin holds a meaning that may surprise. As virgin, she holds the power to bathe herself in the pure waters and arise renewed. This is the virgin power of a forest's *verdant renewal* in nature: to be reborn and renewed with grace and beauty.

THE MESSAGE from the Black Virgin is ~

You have the freedom to be your unique self and create a life that is beautiful and magical in its authenticity.

With her eyes, she sees into the truth of your being. She asks you to love who you are, and to shine the light of your truth and beauty into the world.

She is witness to the pains and suffering of the human condition, and she represents the human face of the empowered feminine presence.

She is the protector of those in childbirth, and also of pregnancy, sex, and marriage.

Is she the pathway to commune with the mystery of life? Is she black because her wood has been charred in the flames of fire, the alchemical element of transformation?

If we relate to blackness without fear, we can get to know this realm and we understand how deep it leads us into our soul. Darkness holds a gift ~ the mystery of creative source.

THERE ARE patterns emerging in the Black Virgins stories as I search to find a truly ancient statue of La Vierge Noire.

Although she is sometimes invisible to the masses, there is a quiet power and an undeniable presence. She seems to speak to me of the ways in which society has related to the dark mysteries of the sacred feminine and all her creative, nurturing, healing, and wise powers. She understands the evolutionary consciousness that lies hidden in matter, the healing power of nature and the true meaning of love.

Like her, I have become familiar with the path within darkness and learned to trust in the natural processes of initiation and incubation that allow a creative impulse to develop and rebirth into new forms.

I have learned to see with new eyes, venturing below the surface into the core of unspoken truths.

I have learned to trust in my spirit guides, my intuition and the way the world mirrors who I am back to me. In short, I have learned to trust in myself.

Healing comes from being seen and loved for who we are in the core essence of our being.

TODAY, a new era is dawning and stories of Mary Magdalene and others are resurfacing, bringing a resurgence of the history of the feminine into consciousness. This resurgence is asking us to change our relationship to all that is dark and mysterious, including the ways of the feminine and to the creative potentiality of our soul essence.

THE MESSAGE CARRIED by the Black Virgin and Child statues

is needed in the world today. She is a symbol of the hidden feminine and is connected to the underground stream, the rivers, and the seas. She reverberates with our psyche (soul) when we are in times of transition. She speaks to us with an inner voice and she has an ancient connection to Lilith, Kali, Mary Magdalene, and many other faces of the sacred feminine as cosmic soul. I am seeing darkness as a gift and her invitation to go within.

In Poland, she is called Our Lady of Czestochowa and openly honoured as the Protectress of Poland. There, she is credited with having miraculous protective and healing powers.

In Montserrat, Spain she is known as Our Lady of Montserrat, "the dark little one," and is revered as a miracle-working statue and patroness of the outcast gypsies.

Blackness contains beginnings and potential hidden within matter and the alchemical healing powers of nature. Alchemy derives from "khem," meaning "black earth"—a symbol of dark creative potential.

It is time for me to leave and as I begin to make my way home to New Zealand, I carry with me an experience of the Black Virgin, which is as empowering as it is mysterious and she has spoken to me of the true meaning of love.

It is all misty this morning in Quillan, and I realise that I love this season of autumn. Not only the colours, but the quietness, the letting go, the gentle warm glow of light, the soft rain, and misty mountains. It is the emotions of these autumn colours that resonate deeply within my soul.

I am now in the autumn of my life and it feels good to begin to know myself and to love myself for who I truly am. Having met La Vierge Noire, I have developed a relationship with blackness that has become a source of healing for me. She has asked me to love the truth of who I am, to shine the light of my beauty and truth into the world, and to trust in the subtle realms and unseen forces of universal intelligence.

*As my conscious awareness of the black feminine grows,
I begin to see La Vierge Noire in places where she is
openly honoured as a healing goddess*

PART V

THE FEMININE: PORTAL TO THE WORLD'S SOUL

The Sacred Creatrix

She is small, she is black, she has a beauty all her own
There is truth in her eyes and simplicity in her form
She lives in a world of unseen forces

She understands the mysteries of birth and death
And sees the hidden gold in the heart of every soul
She is the great mother, Creatrix of all life forms

Her greatest works are done in the darkness
She is patient, she knows how to
be still and to sit and wait
For she is incubating her next creation

There is a magic and mystery to her presence
A depth of wisdom and inner knowing
She sees the beauty in all things and loves
The natural flow of energy we call life

She hears beyond the words that are spoken
She sees into the truth of all matter and
she loves the unique essence of your Being

She is love personified, which heals all things
She embraces you with her wisdom and grace
She is alchemy, the presence of the soulful feminine
She is the Creatrix of all that is

HISTORY: HER-STORY

TO FULLY EMBODY the Creatrix in my life, I first take a look backwards into the patterns around the feminine principle that have arisen out of events in history.

It is these patterns, which have shaped my relationship to the feminine and her powers. This past has also quieted my ability to be heard and valued for expressing my feminine perspective. It explains my shyness and my reticence in owning my full magnetic feminine presence or allowing my soul-self to shine.

I RE-CONNECT to stories of my ancestors and the her-story of women who claimed their power in times gone by, and I recognise that society's relationship to all that is feminine has been overlaid with heavily negative connotations.

Feminine powers have been denigrated, labeled as evil, and feared by many. This has resulted in the disempowerment of feminine ways, and an over emphasis of the masculine.

Wars and the destruction of our lands have been the outcome, and most recently, the wave of refugees fleeing their homelands as a result of wars based on the control of wealth, ethnic cleansing and religious differences.

The effect of this has been the disenfranchisement of thousands of children, and the denial of their right to live in safe and loving homes.

It was when I sat by the river in Alet-les-Bains many years ago that I realised ~ *I believed myself to be a lost soul.*

I felt an overwhelming sadness that I had always carried, which was so much a part of my being that I was not aware of how deep that sadness was. I now believe that the sadness I carried was not just mine, but that of generations of women in my family line: stories of being uprooted from their homeland and never returning, dying young before entering their wisdom years, unable to enjoy their grandchildren. I carry their feelings of deep loss. There is also another layer of sadness that comes from the memories of past histories.

THERE WAS a time as early as 585AD in Burgundy, France, when the myth began to circulate that women did not have a soul. That myth later sparked a series of traumatic events that began with the witch burnings. These memories have had a lasting effect on the psyches of many in todays world.

In the thirteenth century, the inquisitions began a scourge throughout Europe, resulting in huge numbers of women being tortured and violently put to death. Many of them were the midwives, healers, and wise women of the day. This was a time when the feminine became openly denigrated as evil and her powers were feared by many.

BEFORE THIS TIME, wise women were empowered in their role. They were prophetic visionaries and mystics who mediated the transitions of birth and death as physicians of the people.

They were also healers with knowledge of how to use plants to heal, and they held a place of leadership in their communities.

> Memories of these punishing times have impacted us all, resulting in the suppression of feminine wisdom in a strongly patriarchal society.

Six generations of children saw their mothers labeled as evil witches and burned at the stake. This has left scars upon our psyches and brought pain to our souls.

WE ARE BEGINNING to recognise how we have learned to devalue, demonise, and show contempt for feminine values for hundreds of years, and this has been devastating not only for women but for men as well.

This great suffering has resulted in cumulative losses to our flora, our fauna, our people, and the earth. The collective grief that lives within the psyches of men and women echoes our experience of a lost connection to our personal soul, which reflects the lack of honouring the essence of the sacred creative feminine within us all.

MY FASCINATION with the Black Virgin and Child called into question my beliefs around the feminine, as I searched for her statues all over France. Now, I see how she is honoured, protected, and worshipped in France.

The Black Virgin represents the primal essence of the sacred feminine and her mysteries. That she is so often found in the darkness of the crypts of churches reflects the position she has held in society.

She is thought of as a protector, healer, and wise guide by many, and I relate to her as a tangible expression and archetypal symbol of dark feminine powers.

She has been an often invisible symbol; now she is showing herself as heart intelligence that comes from soul with the power to bring a renewed awareness of the feminine into our consciousness. Grace, wisdom and unconditional love are the qualities of her presence.

In Barcelona, the Black Virgin statue of Montserrat presides over marriage, pregnancy, and childbirth, and she is considered to be the patron saint of abandoned daughters, outcasts, and gypsies. How many of us have felt an affinity with these feminine experiences of invisibility?

Mary Magdalene is honoured at Rennes-le-Château and it is thought that she may be part of Béranger's secret that still remains to this day. Some believe that Mary Magdalene travelled to France, spending time living in the Languedoc.

Love was Mary Magdalene's primary message. She blessed Jesus by anointing his feet with precious oils in preparation for what was to come. As a woman connected to nature, she would have known that oils occur naturally as the protective and healing element of plants. They have hidden powers to nourish, protect and heal, which were recognised as a natural way of healing not just the body, but also the mind, the emotions and the soul.

It is now recognised that Jesus valued Mary Magdalene very highly and shared his message with her as his partner. Similarly, the Catholic Church has recently had a turnaround in the way they recognise Mary Magdalene: she is no longer called a whore but is worshiped as a saint and there is now a feast day held in her honour on 22 July each year.

THE CATHAR, who were also persecuted by the Catholic Church, were subjected to the medieval inquisitions and the few who survived went into hiding underground to survive. The remains of their hilltop castles are still to be found throughout the Languedoc. Theirs was a religion based upon love that may have been influenced by Mary Magdalene's presence in France.

- The Cathar believed we could connect to the experience of God within ourselves without the need of a priest as intermediary.
- They valued women and older women could become Parfaits (spiritual leaders) after having their own family.
- They used poetry, storytelling, and singing to tell their stories.

Many of the written accounts of the Cathar are taken from the records of the inquisitions, which are distorted accounts of words extracted from them under torture.

They believed in a pure and simple life, and the name

Cathar means pure ones

Joan of Arc, another spiritual leader, was guided by voices she heard: voices from an authority outside of the church. After leading France to victory in battle against the English, she was condemned as a witch and heretic and put to death.

Recently, however, there has been a shift in how she is seen by the church, and she has now been elevated to the position of an honoured saint. A recurring theme in our her-story.

THAT WHICH HAS BEEN DENIED, denigrated, and distorted is arising into our consciousness, revealing a renewed and empowered feminine. She brings balance between light and dark, and a new level of consciousness to the surface ~ a feminine consciousness with awareness of subtle mysteries, creativity and the essence of life itself and her essence carries the energy of love.

Darkness and sexual energy have been labeled as evil by our Christian religions. Women have been told that they have no soul and that they could not lead a spiritual life without the mediation of a male priest. This was used as a way of controlling women and taking away their power. Powers that are still there, they have just been hidden underground.

THERE IS a need for us to redress this archetypal imbalance between the masculine and the feminine. These times are calling to us to expand into new archetypes of the feminine as symbols of empowerment. We need to remember all that was lost, and change our values and perceptions, and move toward an acceptance of the mystery of the feminine Creatrix and come into a different relationship to all that is dark, mysterious, and essentially unknowable, as this is the home of feminine empowerment.

Archetypes have the ability to nurture us and enrich our conscious awareness to the fundamental needs of humanity. They show themselves to us through images that may be expressed in myths and statues, or they may arise in our imagery and dreams. They have the ability to awaken the deep longings of our souls, to open us to our inner world, and lead us onto our heroine's path of transformation.

Today, a new era is dawning and stories of Mary Magdalene and other powerful women are resurfacing. This shift in consciousness will require that we come into relationship with the creative potentiality within darkness, and into a relationship with our essential soul essence. The Creatrix is returning to reclaim her empowered feminine presence.

If another person can witness that which is hidden in the darkness within you and recognise your inner truth, this empowers you to validate and become witness to the depths of your own experience.

To nurture our soul, we need to journey inwards and connect with the very human parts of ourselves:

Our instincts (inner drives), intuition (inner knowing),
the physicality of our body (our reality in form),
the singing of our heart (inner passion).

*By connecting with these human parts of ourselves,
this will allow us to gain true resonance with our soul.*

*If we live our lives in congruence with our inner truth,
we also are able to connect to our unique gifts*

as expressions of who we truly are.

The Heroine's Journey requires us to willingly go into the darkness of our inner world. Over time, as we sit with *what is* without the need to change anything, we learn to trust the messages that come to us from deep within. The more we give time to this experience of being witness to our inner self, the stronger these connections grow.

Giving this space and time to perceive through the feminine perspective is how we strengthen and honour the feminine presence within us all. She understands what is real in a heartfelt sense. We need to protect and cherish our inner feminine, and give space for her in our busy lives.

Now is time to honour women and nature as the bringers of new life and children, which are the blessings for our future.

When we allow ourselves the freedom to go within, we open doors for the eternal source of creative energy to flow into our lives. In this way we bring the truth of our hearts into our way of being in the world as we reconnect to the feminine and experience personal empowerment. This process requires that we value time spent **being** as well as **doing**, recognising they are both as meaningful as each other.

Pope Francis, in one of his addresses to women in 2015, is quoted as saying "society's dire need for the 'female soul'" and women's "unique gifts" are needed to enrich our world. With these words, he not only acknowledges that women have a soul, but also that soul is essentially feminine.

I have a desire to become secure in my roots and to value the receptivity and nurturing of my inner feminine. I have come to discover that my soul journey is not just about the lifetime I find myself in. It is about lives of the past and the future.

I am discovering the magic of the feminine and the mystery of all creation as I follow a calling to hear the voices of my soul, by withdrawing and connecting to the waters of life within me that are hidden beneath the surface.

As I share these messages about re-valuing of feminine soul, the world reflects back to me that we are already begun changing the ways in which she is valued.

I feel moments of anger that mask the grief of generations of my feminine ancestry, who suffered just for being born as women

20

LIVING THE CREATRESS

The Creatress

*She who knows how to flow with life and live from
her creative centre, connected to the intelligence
of the universe and the wisdom of her soul*

A Creatress knows how to connect to her creative essence, as well as the intelligence of her body, heart, mind and imagination; she values the earth, and all that lives.

*A woman is beautiful when she stands in her power,
in the lightness and darkness of herself
as Creatress, priestess, and healer.*

She connects to the eternal mysteries and attunes herself to a sacred world found in the invisible and subtle energies of mystery and darkness. She is a healing presence, in touch with cosmic soul.

I remember receiving a message, as the sun warmed through me as I sat meditating beside the Sem Stone :

"I can love being a woman."

THESE WORDS MAY SOUND SIMPLE, but they had a profound effect on me. I knew that although I loved parts of me, I did not enjoy the whole of me. These words from the Creatress spoke directly to my heart. A question hung in the air as I reflected upon her message; a question I now ask you

Do you truly love being a woman?

To answer this truthfully is an essential first step to beginning to love all of yourself in all your feminine ways.

Becoming a Creatress, I now hold the core belief that the invisible realms are as real as the world we can see and touch and I remind myself to ~

Honour that which is sacred to me?
Value the pure essence of my feminine self?
Live a life guided by my soul's wisdom?
Reclaim my unique and authentic self?
Find joy in simplicity, and beauty in my truth?

THE BLACK VIRGIN and Child statues held the key for me to own my unclaimed feminine essence. The Black Virgin and Child personify the physical, earthy presence of the Creatrix. A force that knows the parts of you that you may have lost connection to. She recognises your truth, bringing the freedom to be able to begin again, trusting in the guidance that comes from all forms of intelligence ~

Head, heart, and body wisdom, including
instinctual and emotional intelligence
that is both dark and light,

The Black Virgin statues represent the essence of feminine power that resided within, hidden in the darkest recesses of my soul. She awakens a desire in me to embrace the energy of the Creatress in my everyday life.

Having the ability to set clear boundaries with others has become important part of this, as my intentions gained clarity and I learned to speak my truth.

I remember watching a nature program on TV that showed two walruses having a fight. When the fight was over, it was the walrus who had continually stood his ground who became the one to win the challenge.

Now when I am challenged, I think of myself as becoming the walrus who knows how to stand his ground. For me, this is a way of saying:

> *"I am strong in my resolve and I matter.*
> *Don't mess with me, for I won't back down."*

To claim clear boundaries and set clear intentions with an openness as to how those intentions may manifest begins with giving yourself permission to imagine ~ and believe that your hearts true desires are possible

This unlocks the power of your intention that then feeds the power of your thoughts together with your imagination and sets a chain of actions into motion. This leads to synchronicities unfolding, which can sometimes lead you on a circuitous path. Yet when you look back later, you see your journey has taken you gracefully to exactly where you need to be. This synchronicity is serendipity at work.

It is through a woman's body that every living person has been birthed from the darkness of potentiality. It is this feminine processes within us that guides our bodies, instinctually knowing what to do and how. This is the nature of the feminine intelligence known as body wisdom.

The sacred process that is the creation of new life is an essential expression of the feminine forces of the Creatrix. Manifesting through the Creatress who understands the alchemy of creativity that transforms and nurtures new life in all of its forms.

The strength of the Creatress comes from the force of love that lives within her. She knows how to be fearless and strong; compassionate and gracious; wise and loving. She shines her light and loves her darkness and she knows the ways to nourish her soul.

OVER TIME, I have learned that when I flow with life, I am able to choose how I respond in each new moment. I have learned to take my time and to ponder over the messages that come from subtle ways of knowing that connect me to the flow of energy that is both personal and beyond personal.

The river of life is within us. Our blood is the water of our river as it enters our heart and carries the life-giving elements of food and oxygen throughout our bodies; Our veins, the pathways for our blood are the physical rivers of life in our bodies, just as the rivers that flow across our land are the lifeblood that feeds our earth.

Wherever the Creatrix manifests as a Black Virgin statue; a wellspring, underground lake, or river is often found nearby. I have images of an underground lake and wellsprings of purest waters that have the ability to cleanse and heal my heart as a metaphor for the healing gifts of her presence. When I sit with an open heart, I honour the mystery of my existence within my heart. This is the meeting place where our visible and invisible worlds connect.

The Creatress archetype shines through me and I begin to attract synchronicities with her subtle magnetic energy. As she touches me, I feel a charge of emotions and my heart begins to sing. I glow with the feeling of aliveness and have moments in which I experience the gestalt of wholeness that is love. Similarly, art and music have the ability to touch into my heart, awaken me to something within that I do not fully understand.

The Creatress understands the creative principle that brings new life from the formless realms into form. She experiences creativity as the primary force of nature and she knows her body to be a sacred container, a vessel for life's creations.

She brings the gifts of strength, wisdom, creativity, and clarity as she flows with a dynamic sense of being. She is able to rest in the flow of life with a connection to a strength of self that comes from a deep, wise place within and an openness to all that she truly loves.

> By being in the flow of the river of life,
> with a sense of innocence, spontaneity, and freedom
> to be herself, her creative child within awakens,
> the wise woman sings her songs of love, and
> the Creatress dances to her own rhythm
> in tune with the voices of her soul.

The Creatress is represented by three symbols in the tarot:
Empress ~ the vibration of creativity #3;
Hierophant ~ the vibration of the wise woman #5;
Strength ~ the vibration of the power of love #8.

The Empress represents love and beauty, and she is pregnant with new life, new ideas, and new creations. She has the power to create something totally new which is more than the sum of its parts.

She is the golden **Vierge Enceinté** *(pregnant virgin)*

The Hierophant is the speaker of mysteries. She is a bridge-maker and translator of higher knowledge into everyday language so it may be understood and experienced by others. Hers is the courage to speak her wisdom.

She is **La Vierge Noire** *(the Black Virgin)*

The Strength card shows a female magician who lives in tune with her own inner nature. She has a lemniscate (infinity symbol) over her head, representing her ability to live in harmony with universal principles. Her strength comes from the power of love and her connection to her feminine intelligence. Hers is the courage to love herself and to live guided by her inner knowing of feminine ways.

She is the **Creatress**

The Creatress experiences the alchemy of transformation in her life as a seeker. She has developed a deep connection to her soul and to the wisdom of cosmic soul: She is awakened to knowledge that is **gnosis**; a state of deep knowing that is the truth in her heart and the primal originating energy of source.

∽

I BEGAN my journey feeling that I was a lost soul who set out in search of a sense of home, and I found a place in my heart where I can rest, that is home to my soul.

Now, whenever I am in the south of France, the feminine in me comes alive and my heart dances with a playful joy.

As a Creatress, I now know that creativity is at the very heart of my soul. I feel a light shining from the core of my being, as a glint of light sparkles in my eyes, and a glow of happiness emanates all around me. My soul-light shines like a firefly dancing in the night sky, with the illusiveness of mystery and magic rolled into one.

> *When I embody the presence of the Creatress, my soul-light glows and the world reflects this light back to me*

21

THE CIRCLE COMPLETES

A RETURN HOME TO MY SOUL

THERE IS MORE than we are aware of in our world, contained within invisible realms that is energy of immense potentiality. These forces of universal intelligence exist at the Source of our cosmic world. When we live in a world where people shun darkness, the invisible, the unexplainable, and unknowable, then we live in a world guided by fear.

MY EXPERIENCES of awakening in the southwest of France have led me to uncover the essence of feminine energy as I learned how to live from an inner place centred in feminine wisdom ways that are life giving and hold the power to know and heal our hearts.

In this process of my reclaiming the sacred feminine, I have learned to see her, to know her, and express something of her essential nature. For she is in everything - she is the earth and nature itself; she dwells at the primal level of all existence and I call her the sacred Creatrix.

It is time for new patterns to emerge of both masculine and feminine, and for us to weave a new story. Time to redefine courage as the willingness to face into the unknown and to listen to the feelings in our hearts. Then we can make new choices, create new habits, and use courage as a transformative energy to perceive with different eyes, listen in different ways and to relate to each other with love.

Darkness has become my friend; for it is in the silence of solitude that I connect to my soul-self. I hear voices from this inner place which guide me to know and live my truth.

I understand the masculine as spirit and feminine as soul that both exist within us all. Spirit provides structures and is focused on action while the soul provides nurturing and the ability to create form out of formlessness. They are both modes of the aliveness of energy in motion. It is time for these two polarities to be fully appreciated.

There is a place in Toulouse where three rivers meet, and there is a place within me where three worlds meet. This is where the visible, the hidden, and the invisible worlds converge. I no longer fear the unknowable or the unseen realms, and at times, I have felt an intimate connection with universal energy of Source. Some call this becoming part of the consciousness of Humanity.

I know my heroine's journey as my path to becoming a Creatress. I travelled to France many times, and each time something of my feminine nature has been nourished. My awakened soul opened me to the vulnerable parts of myself so that I could discover what truly matters to me. I have learned to let go of old sorrows and disappointments, and to go into the forest (for rest) to find peace. I have learned to sit with stillness and to connect into the aliveness within me and I have released the guilt I originally felt when I first began to take time out to be with myself.

I now make choices by listening to my heart, and my inner intuitive voice has grown strong and clear. It is a voice that is wise and loving and I live from a place of trust in my inner knowing and I connect with my Hestia goddess to shine my own light and honour the sacredness of my life.

MAGIC HAPPENS when I live in the flow life, listening to my heart and the other voices that are my soul-speak. As I simplify my life, I connect to the core of my being and experience a dynamic sense of aliveness. I feel my inner strength and become open to all I truly love.

My quest has been to own the beauty, power and creativity of the Feminine energy within me. I have faced challenges along my path and have stepped beyond my fears to find my courage. My trust in life has grown and I am able to honour the Creatress within me in important ways:

1. Surrendering to the flow, becoming lost, and being guided by listening to the voices of my soul.
2. Honouring my body as the ground of my being, and my emotions as expression of my heart.
3. Learning to trust my inner knowing and allowing it to guide me ~ as my intuition grows stronger and my path grows clearer.
4. Trusting with patience, knowing that my true path unfolds and reveals itself to me in its own

time. I allow myself to connect to my past and to my future and be present in this moment in time.
5. As I develop the feminine qualities of receptivity, softness, and gently flowing movements, creative processes unfold and my truth is reflected back to me in beautifully synchronistic ways.
6. My feminine self knows how to be strong and fierce when it needs to be. I can stand my ground and speak my truth and defend my boundaries.
7. I discovered my fierce, protective feminine instinct when I had young children and I knew that if needed, this force within me would be willing to fight to the death to protect them. I also know that I can put away my sword too, for I rarely need to use it now that my boundaries are strong and clear, and my voice is true.
8. My emotions speak to my heart and they align me with the truth hidden in my soul.
9. I am able to connect to a symbolic life that honours the sacredness of all things and carries the power to heal my soul.
10. I give myself permission to love being a woman in all her subtle, complex and mysterious ways.

LIVING a life of soul is healing to my heart and illuminates my personal path with feelings of rightness, and happiness arise within me. They bubble up from a place of pure joy that comes from living in the flow of life. I am committed to honouring the sacred feminine as a loving, wise, and healing force, and I now trust in her guidance every day of my life.

My journey taught me many lessons as I came to uncover a new awareness of the limitlessness love, wisdom and healing of the sacred feminine. I learned the language of my heart that speaks to me from the source essence of the Creatrix.

I have become a seeker of truth, expanding my connection to the physical world, the psychic realms, and the oneness of source energy. For me this is the process of revaluing the sacred feminine at a primal level of my existence.

I now know that my heart connects me to the deepest, darkest truth of who I am in my very essence at the core of my being that exists as the intelligence of my soul.

I HAVE NEEDED to heal past traumas by confronting the pain I carried in my heart. My awareness of the deep sadness I had inherited ~ personally, ancestrally, and collectively became a turning point in my healing process. I allowed myself to sit in the sadness that I had learned from my mother. Moments when anger erupted from a deep place within me, forced me to be real and true with myself as I recalled my mother's anger too, that was born from an intensity of emotions that seemed beyond my reasoning. I was releasing a deep well of grief, which I had been carrying for many lifetimes.

The intensity of my emotions sometimes scared me. It was an expression of a guttural cry of pain from the depths of my soul, and the souls of my ancestors. From this place, I learned to sit with the not-knowing of these experiences and wait for a new awareness to come to me. To do this, I needed to stay in the quiet of the moment with aliveness to what arises.

I needed to give myself permission to feel the depths of my emotions in a very personal way and to be kind to my feminine self. To trust in the information which my instincts and emotions bring to me is to go against the training of my rational logos mind.

To allow my emotions to be validated as meaningful and real is to be able to live in the river's flow and the ocean's currents of my life.

Emotions need to be felt as waves of energy that arise into consciousness; just as the ocean greets the sandy shores or the river's flow caresses the riverbank. These waves move on to become one with the great unconscious realms.

In time, I discovered I had choices in the way I expressed the stories of my past. I could make them grow in presence and overwhelm me, or I could remember them, imagine them floating onto a cloud outside of myself, and let them go. As I did so, I began to feel a rush of creativity enter me. I learned to laugh again, to sing and dance. I set my soul free to soar like a bird above the clouds and return to me again.

I feel released to begin to create another story, one that nourishes my feminine soul. By changing the images that we carry within us, we can change our lives. It was through this journey that I began to understand and be guided by the language of my soul.

THE CIRCLE IS the feminine principle of the cycles in nature. The circle can also become a spiral, that shifts us to a higher level of consciousness. When we come together in circles, we create a place where we can show our vulnerability, share stories, enjoy camaraderie and explore the mystery and magic of life.

There is a strength that comes from the path of inner reflection. Knowing with a beginner's mind gives a sense of the innocent spontaneity of childlike wonder that provides the courage to fully live our truth from a place of love.

THE CIRCLE COMPLETES

THE WORLD IS SUFFERING a general malaise that comes from a loss of connection to soul. My hope is that this story will help others to open the door to their personal sense of soul so that their hearts can sing their unique song of joy. It is my hope that they can live more fully from their creative essence and their connection to the cosmic soul that reaches into the past and the future and is alive within us all.

We can restore meaning in our lives by the simple acts of loving the feminine within us and taking the time to honour the voices of our soul. Our truth is written in our hearts and is the expression of our soul and our soul connects us to the source energy where the cosmic soul resides.

MY JOURNEY HAS LED me to a deeper relationship to myself and guided me to live from a place of soul and has allowed me the space and time to connect to the creative energies within me. My life has become a creative symphony in rhythm with my truth. I can be passionate and strong; sensitive and vulnerable; and I respect and trust in the invisible realms.

We are being called to honour the earth and all that exists upon it, and to find ways for the feminine to be in authentic relationship with the masculine without losing connection to her feminine ways of wisdom, that are the ways of soul.

My journey has taken me from feeling lost, to uncovering the richness of feminine wisdom within me and becoming an empowered soulful woman connected to the pure creative essence of the feminine.

I hear the music in my heart that is my soul's song. The

yin and yang of life come into harmony when the Creatrix and the Creator can both live within us, valuing each other equally and honouring the earth as the ground of our being.

> *The sacred feminine reawakens into my world*
> *and my soul's golden glow lights my way*

22

THE ESSENCE OF FEMININE SOUL

The Creatrix is the feminine counterpart to the masculine Creator, and as such, she is pure creative energy of the feminine that arises from cosmic source.

"The Creatrix is she-who-creates."

- *She is the feminine principle*
- *She is the alchemy of nature*
- *She creates from source and the primordial darkness of the great, unknowable cosmic realms*
- *She is connected to the intelligence of source*
- *She symbolises the potentiality within blackness that emanates from the originating matrix of Source*

SHE IS cosmic feminine soul ~ a feminine creative force that resides within the dark oceans of potentiality. Her domain is the realm of the great unconscious, veiled in mystery.

The processes of alchemy is her natural way of continuously coming into form and dissolving back into formlessness.

She flows in tune with nature as she moves from darkness into light; from the invisible into the visible; and from the unknowable into the knowable.

She creatively manifests, she receives all and brings forth all.

The Creatrix has the power to transform energy into physical and soul presence. Honouring her creative force brings us moments when we feel a rightness to life: a grace, a beauty, and a sense of fulfilment and joy.

THE VIERGE NOIRE and myth of Psyche symbolise the physical presence of the sacred feminine and tell us her stories. Our task is only to become conscious of her mystery and creativity when she enters our lives.

A way to perceive the essence of the Creatrix ~

Three dimensions of the Feminine
The visible, invisible and cosmic dimensions
the Black Virgin , Psyche and Creatrix
~ See the table included after this chapter.

The Creatrix shows up as her personification of La Vierge Noire as an earthy presence ; and her soul presence as the mythic story of Psyche. Her cosmic dimension that is beyond the invisible is the mystical presence of the Creatrix.

We may occasionally get to glimpse her invisible dimension in brief moments in time; the source energy of the Creatrix reveals itself to us in numinous moments and through the mystery of *the alchemy of becoming.*

A CREATRESS IS the archetypal expression of the Creatrix.

She has the ability to create new life out of very little. A work of art, a book, a beautiful meal: she takes simple ingredients and creates something much greater from them. Birthing new forms in nature is a natural expression of this feminine principle, transitioning from invisible into visible, just as the monthly cycles of the moon as she reveals her light.

Her language is that of body talk, instincts, emotions and imagination. She speaks to us through our connection to our heart. Her messages come to us as physical sensations, emotional reactions, intuitions, inspirations and psychic knowing. In these ways we connect to intelligence of Source.

The Creatrix understands the cycles of becoming and dissolving. She knows the importance of time spent in incubation, re-forming new life before calling on masculine that expresses through action and outer achievement.

The Creatrix is an essential force of the universe; and the ground from which all is created; and her beauty can be found in the simplest of things.

The brightness of the moon and stars in the night sky which needs the darkness to be able to shine, is the healing quality of the velvet black feminine that contains the mystery and magic of feminine soul.

The feminine soul is illusive, magical, and is the mystery of life itself. A receptive energy of magnetic attraction that is both personal and universal; and has a soul wisdom that can bring a deep quality of meaning to our lives. The presence of the Creatrix is a magnetic force that is subtle, gentle, and intensely powerful.

Water is the natural element of feminine soul.

WATER IS in everyone and is everywhere. It is the first essential element for life as we know it to exist. It can mix with other elements and flow into any form. or it can be one as the great body of the oceans or the rivers. When it mixes with air, it can take on different forms: it is the froth at the edge of a wave, the mist in the morning air, or a dark cloud, heavy with rain.

The moon affects the rise of the tides and the flow of water within us, and is most powerful when she shines at the full moon when she is her brightness in the night sky. At this time she is farthest way from the sun, and her magnetic pull is strongest ~ the tides rise higher and the water within us rises too, and our emotions intensify within us.

The moon symbolises the mother and the child, and describes how we nurture and feed ourselves emotionally. Being in the flow of the river or bathing in pure spring waters is a way to feel reborn into the sacred energy of the feminine.

I have grown to know the Creatrix as connection to Source and as I express from this place I become a Creatress. Perhaps this archetype could be called the "sourceress," as she manifests from the source energy of the universe.

MY INTUITION HAS BECOME my inner guide. I take time to incubate and assimilate before new words surface into my consciousness. Guidance comes to me in its own time, often arriving as complete sentences at moments when I least expect them and notice my energy as it resonates with the world around me.

Words come to me out of nowhere, as if on angels' wings.

My intuition flashes into my consciousness with a feeling of truth is different from the messages of my dreamtime. As my connection to my inner wisdom grows, I often experience this deep truth resonating at the level of my soul.

When we know the truth of who we are, we take on the task of expressing our truth. We become aware of the power of our thoughts and intentions and we find ourselves living from a place of authenticity and synchronicity abounds as we express ourselves from the essence of our personal soul.

ABOVE ALL, I believe that the pure essence of the Creatrix is primal potentiality; a dimension that exists beyond our everyday consciousness. She is the feminine face of Source and the core essence of creative feminine power.

By expanding my awareness to the cosmos within me,
I glimpse my connection to the creative energy of Source

Three Faces of the Feminine

Visible	Hidden	Invisible
Heart	Soul	Cosmic Soul
Beauty	Truth	Potentiality
Love	Healing	Creativity
Magic	Mystery	Matrix
Black Virgin	Psyche	Creatrix

Qualities of the Feminine

Shining	Glowing	Darkness
Light	Shadow	Blackness
Full Moon	Dark Moon	Black Moon
Charisma	Magnetic	Holograms
Open Heart	Vulnerability	Boundless
Inspiration	Incubation	Pre-Birth
Presence	Transformation	Beyond Death
Heart	Soul	Creativity
Love	Healing	Alchemy
Body Wisdom	Intuition	Soul guidance

POSTSCRIPT:

MY JOURNEY HOME

I have always held a strong desire to live an authentic life, and over time this has grown into a need to live a life of soul. My soul feels very new and very ancient at the same time, and its realms are subtle and mysterious. It connects me to memories of past incarnations as well as intuitions of my future.

I have learned to step lightly on my path and to listen in ways that reach beyond my mind. I have learned that there are forces greater than myself that can guide me if I allow them to do so. I have chosen a path of individuation, which has led me to a greater sense of my soul. I now feel compassion, love, and forgiveness for my imperfect self.

Below are some ways in which I foster the presence of the feminine in my everyday life:

I have learned to sit in my truth and face my fear of owning my feminine power by becoming the Creatress of my life. The Creatress is my inspiration—the breathing in of life.

I am happiest when I am living creatively and trust in the intuitive messages that come to me, for claircognisance is my psychic gift.

Sleep time has become invaluable for me, as time to let go so that the great unconscious can do its work. I start my day by waking slowly and sitting quietly so I can hear my soul speaking to me. While in that semi-relaxed state between sleeping and wakeful activity, I catch the first words that enter my consciousness. I always have a large notepad beside my bed to record any intuitions that are there upon waking.

I protect and nurture my energy field, honouring the sensitive, intuitive person I have become. Qigong, Reiki and essential oils are ways in which I nurture my sensitivity to energy fields. They support me to live in a state of conscious awareness to the energies in the world around me.

I also go for beach walks, which connect me to the elements and raise my chi energy. Beach walks are a meditation with my eyes open, a time in which I am present to the energies of the moment. They allow me to live in the current of life, flowing like water. Being open and relaxed, I let go and breathe deeply. This brings me to a place of peace within.

Whenever I need to, I give myself a soul health day without any guilt. Having felt the urgency of my soul to be heard, I have come to treasure my time spent in open-ended reflection. This consists of totally unplanned time out with space to focus on my experiences of being present as an observer of my life in contrast with my daily experience of being "in" my life.

I have learned how to ride the waves of my emotions as they arise like swells from the deep oceans of my life. I have dived into the hidden depths within and let the waves wash over and through me. As they do, they change me and deepen my relationship to the hidden depths within my soul.

As they move away, I feel more real and more alive, and I allow the energy of my truth to move through me and bring a new consciousness to the surface of my awareness.

I honour the sacredness of life in the way I live every day, staying in touch with my inner sacred flame and with the magical glow of aliveness that is natural, real, spontaneous, and loving. I become virgin each day as I sit in silence and renew my connection to the energy of source. I now give myself permission to acknowledge my emotions and instincts as valid information that comes from a place that is natural and feminine. I have learned to tune into the rhythm of the cosmos and flow with its music and to enter a space where personal soul, collective soul, and cosmic soul meet.

Ultimately, I know that the experience of being an outsider has given me the freedom to find my own, unique voice and create my individual path in life. I have created a new story for myself and have learned to live my life as a Creatress. My ability to experience joy in the simplest things has brought my life moments of true happiness. I now find myself with more time for my inner life and this allows me to live in deep connection with my soul.

As I embrace the Creatress in my life, I become grounded and healed. The river song has become a love song from my soul, guiding me to love myself as I am and feel the strength, power and beauty of the Creatress within me.

"As soon as you trust yourself, you will know how to live."
— Johann Wolfgang von Goethe

GLOSSARY

cosmic soul. Universal wisdom is always present in a dimension where the invisible and the unknowable realms meet, and where the mystery of creative potentiality resides. This is the home of the cosmic soul, which contains memories of past and future for everything we will ever know.

creatress. The Creatress personifies the creative feminine principle that is loving and wise. She knows how to flow with life and live from her creative centre, connected to the intelligence of our universe as source and the wisdom of her soul. The Creatress lives in tune with her truth as she shines the essence of her unique creative self into the world. The Creatress connects us with the earth and all living things through the wisdom of her body, heart, and intuitive mind. When the Creatress is present, the feminine ways of being and knowing and the sacredness of life come together.

creatrix. The word "Creatrix" is the feminine version of the word "Creator." She is the feminine counterpart of the masculine creator. She is pure and primal creative energy that arises from source.

feminine principle. The feminine exists within all of us and is expressed through the elements of earth and water. Her presence manifests as expressions of love as she births her creations into physical form through the archetype of the Creatress. She embraces the mystery and the sacredness of life as the alchemy of becoming.

gnosis. Gnosis, the Greek word for knowledge, is the earth's most ancient form of religion. To know as gnosis is to hear the wisdom of the soul that speaks through the heart and is the secret knowledge of all things hidden. It is the path of insight and inner reflection that leads one to self-knowledge, a knowledge that can set one free. In its purest form, it is intuitive spiritual knowledge that comes to us from a direct communion with the intelligence of source.

personal soul. This personally felt sense of soul has the power to connect to the intelligence of physicality, stored memories of the ancient past, and the future in potentiality. It is an innate wisdom that brings meaning to one's life. The personal soul creates a bridge between the wisdom in the heart and the wisdom of the universe (cosmic soul).

source. The matrix of primal energy from which all matter originates through the alchemy of becoming. It is the invisible realm of universal consciousness where the primary forces of the Creatrix exist as pure, undifferentiated consciousness beyond the space-time continuum.

ACKNOWLEDGMENTS

Thank you to my children, Jeremy and Marnie, who have kept me real and grounded. Having them in my life has been a gift beyond words and has brought me much happiness.

Thanks to my granddaughters, Emelie and Sofia who were born far away in Sweden. I was there when you were born and I now have the joy of seeing you grow into beautiful, creative young women.

To Merryn José, my soul sister, who has always believed in me, even when I didn't believe in myself. Thank you for our many phone conversations and your loving support.

To Suzanne Glendinning who has been my long-time friend, and with whom I have shared travels in France: may we keep travelling and laughing together.

To Franchelle Ofsoské-Wyber who reminded me of my true path and who became the first reader of my book. Thanks for your sensitive feedback on my first draft and our many astrological conversations.

Lynda Craven, who I met in cyberspace and who became my second reader. Thanks for all those late night and early morning discussions.

To Carina Karlsson, who has welcomed me to stay in her home on my many visits to Sweden—thank you for our ritual morning conversations over coffee and for joining me on my visit to Montsegur in France.

A huge thank you to my editor, Erena Shingade, for all her help and support. She gave me clear direction every step of the way and has added her professional touch beautifully.

Lastly, I would like to thank the unconscious realms for the many nightly wakeup calls at 3am when words would arrive flowing in complete sentences, and to Mimi my dog, who often still wakes me at 3am as a habit formed over the years.

ABOUT THE AUTHOR

Madeline K Adams is an intuitive, a dancer, and a seeker of soul. She writes from her Aquarian perspective, guided by her intuition and the creative intelligence of her soul.

Madeline holds a B. Comm. degree with postgraduate studies in psychology. She has studied archetypal psychology and astrology for over three decades.

Astrology describes the ever-changing cosmos in symbolic form, giving her a universal language to show with beauty, grace, and elegance; a blueprint of the complex and dynamic energies of each unique soul.

On her first visit to France at the age of seventeen, Madeline instantly felt a soul connection. Many years later, her experiences in France stirred something deep within her psyche that initiated her quest for a heartfelt connection to her feminine wisdom and to know herself as soul.

Madeline is the Creatress of the Source and Soul Series.
She lives in Auckland, New Zealand.

Visit her websites:
www.sourceandsoul.com
www.madelinea.com

 facebook.com/SourceandSoul

SOURCES AND FURTHER READING

Below is a list of books that have greatly influenced the writer, some of which have been quoted from in the text. This list may also offer you direction for further reading.

Arroyo, Stephen. *Astrology, Psychology, and the Four Elements: An Energy Approach to Astrology and Its Use in the Counseling Arts.*
CRCS Publications, 1975.

Begg, Ean. *The Cult of the Black Virgin.*
Penguin Books, 1996.

Brennan, Barbara. *Hands of Light: A Guide to Healing Through the Human Energy Field.*
Bantam Books, 1988.

Ferrucci, Piero. *What We May Be: Techniques for Psychological and Spiritual Growth Through Psychosynthesis.*
Jeremy P. Tarcher, Inc., 1982.

Greer, Mary. *Tarot Constellations: Patterns of Personal Destiny.*
Newcastle Publishing, 1987.

Jung, Carl. *Memories, Dreams, Reflections*.
Flamingo/Fontana Paperbacks, 1983.

Sasportas, Howard. *The Gods of Change: Pain, Crisis, and the Transits of Uranus, Neptune, and Pluto*.
Arkana, 1989.

Woodman, Marion. *The Pregnant Virgin: A Process of Psychological Transformation*.
Inner City Books, 1985.

ALSO BY MADELINE K. ADAMS

The Sacred Dance of Soul
Your Inner Journey to Empowerment

Soul Star ~ Child of the Universe
Soul Poems and Heart Wisdom

Visit Madeline's website sourceandsoul.com where you can click on Gallery to see Madeline's story come alive with images of the places she visited and treasures she found on her travels to France.

- The Black Virgin Statues
- L'Enciente
- The Sem Stone
- The church at Rennes le Chateau

Join our Source and Soul Community
www.sourceandsoul.com

Visit www.madelinea.com
For Inspiration and Soul wisdom

One Last Thing.....

If you enjoyed this book or found it useful, I'd be very grateful if you could post a short review at your preferred retailer.

Your support really does make a difference. I read all the reviews personally, so I can get your feedback and make my next book even better.

Thanks again for your support!

Madeline K Adams

www.ingramcontent.com/pod-product-compliance
Lightning Source LLC
Chambersburg PA
CBHW021949290426
44108CB00012B/997